# The Elevation
of the
*Femalepreneur*

Volume 2

Copyright © JoJo Ellen and Natasha Edwards 2020

JoJo Ellen and Natasha Edwards have asserted their right to be identified as the authors of this Work in accordance with the Copyright, Designs and Patents Act 1988.

All rights reserved.
No part of this publication may be reproduced, stored in a retrieval system, or transmitted in any form or by any means, electronic, mechanical, photocopying, recording or otherwise, without the prior permission of the copyright owner.

Typeset by Fuzzy Flamingo
www.fuzzyflamingo.co.uk

Robert Wilkinson: @bobteddy.co.uk
Jordan Hayes studio: www.jordanhayesstudio.com
Andrea De Haan, AH image studio:
https://ahimagestudio.com/about/

A catalogue for this book is available from the British Library.

# Contents

| | |
|---|---|
| How Not to Parent: *Amy Morelli Barnes* | 1 |
| Never Lose Sight of Your Vision: *Anita Barzey* | 7 |
| Series of Events! *Becky Kennedy* | 16 |
| Your Life, Your Responsibility: *Carla Maria* | 25 |
| The Gardener and the Flower: *Casey Bird* | 35 |
| You Control Your Future: *Claire Maynard* | 44 |
| Breaking Free from the Voices in Your Head: *Debbie Patrick* | 51 |
| Listen to the Story of Your Soul: *Elly Charles* | 59 |
| Always Believe In Your Soul: *Helen Adams* | 69 |
| Why Me? *Katie Yarham* | 79 |
| For the Silent Voices: *Katy Curry* | 90 |

Things Can Always Get Better: *Leanne Willis*     100

From Surviving to Thriving: *Lyndsey Shelley*     108

Life is for Living – Don't Settle for a Life Less Than You Deserve! *Martha Bradford*     116

The Road To Light: *Melanie Jack*     128

The Fire Within: *Monique Sveinsson*     138

# How Not to Parent
## Amy Morelli Barnes

*This chapter is dedicated to my children, Jacob, the boy who made me a mother first, George, who showed me how to laugh at nothing, and Rosie, my little devil dressed as an angel. I hope you will be proud of me and what I have written. I would like to also dedicate this chapter to my mum, Donna Morelli. Thank you for raising me by yourself and showing me how to be strong, I love you. Last but not least, to my husband Rian Barnes. Thank you for helping make these three gorgeous babies and being their dad.*

Hello, my name is Amy Morelli Barnes. I am a single mum to three beautiful babies and I really don't like them.

Did she just open her chapter with 'she doesn't like her kids'? Surely not.

I have for a long time felt like I failed my kids. I've felt like I'm not enough for them and don't deserve to be their mum.

Just recently I've only been able to fully open up about my fears as a parent, my worries and, more than anything, the big A word in our home. AUTISM.

Jacob, the eldest, was diagnosed at the age of three with ASD (autism spectrum disorder), which is about to be amended to ADHD, sensory sensitivity and global development delay. We, as a family, struggled to come to terms with "what's wrong" with Jacob and even longer to adapt to the very difficult battles we face every single day. The middle child, George, is as I'm writing this going through the process of a diagnosis. Yes, both boys are autistic. We then have the third child, my exact personality double and my karma, Rosie. She is what you would class the normal child with absolutely no additional needs.

Now you know the background, maybe the start isn't as harsh. Still? Okay, bear with me.

The night I'm sitting here writing this, I woke in the morning to my bed saturated in milk as Rosie was slightly off target with her bottle. Jacob had completely demolished a massive bag of chocolates and George had emptied my entire make up and destroyed it all. Did I mention this was all before 6:30am? This was followed by tantrums, tears, mood swings and Jacob giving himself a full on nosebleed

Now you are with me! Welcome to my world!

The first sentence is also complete horse waste. I truly believe everything in our lives, the good the bad and the complete and utter ugly, happens for a reason. You are meant to learn and grow. You are in this battle because guess what, you can do it. Parenting is the absolute hardest part of adult life but MY GOD the most rewarding in every single way. I'm that mum who shouts and screams and gives them nuggets on days I don't fancy cooking. I'm also that mum who dances in the kitchen with them, cooks them amazing meals and lets them go out into the garden and eat mud – and yes that's their dinner sometimes.

I suppose what I'm trying to say is, it doesn't matter who you are or what you look like, you are most probably the best parent your kids could ever need. My mum reminds me that kids don't know any other love but ours. They are not materialistic and don't want anything but your love. So why do we put pressure on ourselves so much? If that's all they need, why do we question absolutely everything we do?

Tell you why: because we want the best for them, we want them to have it all and be the best-behaved children ever. Reality check – even you, Insta mum – no one is perfect. Absolutely no one. You will never be perfect, but your imperfections make your lives so much more interesting.

You know what the craziest part about this is? I'm the absolute best at giving advice but I won't ever take my own. I wrote the top 500 words in a time I thought yes, I'm getting somewhere in life, I mean check me out, I'm in a freaking book! Amy from Strood, Kent, who loves her crisp sandwiches and secretly eats like a pig. (This stays between you and me reading this chapter.) But then life came to test me yet again. This time I really thought I'd lost. Lost my head, my battle, trying to do the best I can and even the person I started to become. I then open my Word document to my little chapter and read it back and think to myself, "Ames! You got this, Queen!"

So, where were we? Ahh yes, I don't like my kids.

When it all boils down to it, it doesn't matter if you are a stay-at-home mum or a mum who works all the hours under the sun. If you're a full-time dad or only see your children at weekends. You – and I'm talking to you directly – you are a parent. You made that lovely little baby and now you have full responsibility, not just for eighteen years, but forever. Your only job is to raise that little baby to be a wonderful person. Full of good manners, good morals and just a little bit of hygiene skills would be helpful. If you have managed to get your baby to expert hygiene skills my hat goes off to you. Of course, if you choose to multiply, from one parent to another, I totally feel you and get why you may be on the verge of your brain fully melting into slush.

Opening up about your fears as a parent is absolutely terrifying. Makes me think, "God, if I really tell anyone my thoughts and what goes through my head, I think social services would be called!" I promise you now that when you do open up, that parent feels the exact same. I'm lucky to have two mum friends that I can be brutally honest with and every time I say something, they never ever judge. For example, I would say, "I'm going to literally just walk out in a minute!" My friend's reply: "Did that last week, Ames, they still screamed." Please note, no one actually left their children; this was in fact a way for my mum friend to make me laugh when I felt overwhelmed.

The biggest time I ever opened up was on a Facebook live of all places. I never spoke about Jacob's autism openly on social media. I have, from the time of learning Jacob was showing signs of autism, had to push and fight for everything he needed. From professional help to taking him out of a nursery as the manager referred to my son as a "safeguarding issue". I was working in network marketing so posting and doing lives regularly was my job and I wasn't even slightly camera shy. In what can only be described as a rant, I took to a live video after a phone call about my son being refused a school placement for his autism. I had had enough and had it in my head that someone else may just understand, and I wanted the video to be shared to my local government. Well it got back to them all right with over 132,000 views and 2,100 people sharing my little video. With that, I also received a massive number of messages from parents/carers seeking help or advice or just thanking me for speaking out like they haven't seen before. I was offered multiple TV and radio appearances, and requests to appear in papers, and one of my biggest regrets is never accepting these offers and telling my Jacob's story on a higher platform.

What I decided to do instead was to set up my own charity business. One to specify in helping autism families. My vision is to link other charities, authorities and any other form of help to the parents. We fight so hard and have to shout so loud to be heard and that isn't how it should be. I'm still in the very early stages but I'm loving it so far and I've stopped any other forms of business to fully focus on this charity and give it absolutely everything I have.

If I didn't talk to someone, if I didn't go on a rant on Facebook, which took guts, yes, but at the time I was talking directly to the council and how disgusted I was, I wouldn't have my charity business. Because I just let go and spoke my mind, it's paid off with now having a passion I can't stop talking about.

Yes, you're a bad parent and yes you do and say things that will make you feel guilty, but guess what, you're also the best parent ever for just existing and being with your child. I know my chapter isn't long, but I hope this helps you see that we are all in the same boat riding the crazy parent wave. If you ever want to talk please feel free to reach out to me, I'm only a message away.

★★★

You can find Amy here:

https://www.facebook.com/jacobstrust1/

# Never Lose Sight of Your Vision

## Anita Barzey

*I'm dedicating this chapter to all the women who have ever been scared to step into their power. Never lose sight of the vision you have for your life – even when life presents you with obstacles and challenges, never forget that vision. You've got this, I promise.* ♡
*I dedicate this to the mothers juggling so much that sometimes they forget they need to pause – I see you and I appreciate all you do.*
*Thank you to all my family and friends who have ever supported me on my journey and listened to my endless stories and dreams.* ♡
*Life takes a new meaning when you realise how close you were to death.*

As I lay in the all too familiar hospital bed, I tried to piece together the last twelve months. It had been a bittersweet roller coaster of events from becoming a first-time mother to discovering my partner had been hiding big secrets, which ultimately had left me heartbroken. Although I never had a mental breakdown, I most certainly had a physical one. I realised at that moment something had to change, I couldn't carry on this way. My stress levels had been so high that it had triggered my nineteen-year dormant condition intercranial hypertension, also known as IH.

IH had played havoc on my life as a child, leaving me with severe visual impairment. Although waking up completely blind at the age of ten had been such a traumatic time for me and my family, it had been the driving force that had kept me motivated when frankly I had wanted to give up.

As I lay in the hospital bed, I could hear the surgeon telling me the last surgery on my brain had been unsuccessful and that I would be going back down in the morning. It wasn't really sinking in… is this some sick joke? It's 10.30pm at night! No time to prepare myself or even see my family one last time.

I'm not one to give up easily, but I had mentally given up, the fight had left my body. I couldn't fight it this time, I was actually preparing myself to die in the very hospital I was born and where I had also delivered my son the previous year.

What does one do when they think they are about to die? Being practical, I wrote a quick email to my sister and mum outlining what to do if I was to pass and the plans I had for my son. That was hard, but I knew that it was a must. Although I had no time for a legal document, I felt better knowing I had written something. I had prayed the longest prayer of my life and had a really serious talk with God: "Hold on, I'm twenty-eight – too young to die," I cried. Oh boy, did I cry. In all honesty, I had been pretty mad with God, and had been living the last twenty-eight years on autopilot and refusing point blank to have a relationship with Him. I couldn't understand the sight loss – underneath it all I was bitter and angry.

When I really break it down, what was I crying for? I was crying for all the things I was yet to achieve, my poor baby, all the silly mistakes and poor judgements I had made, but the biggest reason I was sobbing my heart out was because I was about to die broke, leaving no legacy for my son.

No way am I leaving the earth this way! You know we all have pivotal moments that shape us, shake us, or damn right push us to our limits? 2017 was that year for me.

No way am I leaving no legacy for my son…

No way, no way, no way.

No way, no way, no way.

Change is on its way

The next few weeks were the most physically and mentally draining weeks of my life. Seven operations, various tests, countless scans and being prodded and poked in all sorts of places. I prayed, I read, journaled, listened to hours of motivational videos and rested. I wanted to leave that hospital a different woman. I was so thankful that God had spared my life. It started a new chapter. I wanted to get better, I was eager to get out of that hospital and create that legacy for my son. I learnt the art of gratitude, I knew that I was one lucky girl to be alive.

### The past has shaped me but not defined me

At the age of ten, I lost my sight and ultimately suffered from years of low self-esteem and a lack of confidence. I tried to hide my disability. Looking back, I had nothing to be ashamed of, but as a young girl wanting to fit in and pretend to the rest of the world that I was as sighted as them, you can imagine I was embarrassed and ashamed of my severe sight loss.

My saving grace was performing. I discovered acting at the age of seven and performing gave me something to be passionate about. I could hide while on stage, whether that be dancing, acting or singing. I used my other senses the majority of the time, and I remembered voices but never faces (many awkward stories which could fill a book).

I left school and, although it had been a struggle, almost a pretence, I enjoyed the experience and made some good friends. Moving onto college was a bit more exciting. Studying performing arts full time was the best two years ever. It was hard work but it was the place that I realised I could achieve almost anything if I worked hard, dreamt big and set goals! I was focused and driven and boys always came second to my performing. An underlying issue was that, although I was excelling in my course, I lacked confidence and that voice kept on telling me I wasn't good enough because of my sight loss. I lived in total fear of deteriorating sight loss and failure.

As my course ended, I embarked on a journey to university to study drama again. This really wasn't the easiest transition for me. I was the first to attend university in my immediate family and my fears of not fitting in were present again. Not only was I moving away from home but I was worried about being honest about my sight loss and my needs. So again I tried to do what I did best and pretend I was sighted and not needing support. Biggest mistake ever! Although I enjoyed uni, I never felt fully fulfilled because I declined help that I needed due to shame. I don't know who needs to hear this but never ever be ashamed to ask for what you need, don't feel silly for needing extra support.

My big wake-up call and 'get your ass together' moment came in 2009 while embarking on a volunteering project in Ghana. It was the best experience of my life and I believe I owe a lot to this experience as it's shaped the teacher and entrepreneur that I am today.

For the first time in my life I had to openly reveal my sight loss to the other fifteen volunteers with whom I shared a house. OMG did I feel empowered and free from shame for the first time in years. I realised I had to say something to protect myself and others. The response from the volunteers was refreshing and I realised it was me with the problem and no one else. I had been creating fictional responses in my mind. I had never grieved for my sight loss and literally tried to get on with my life. While in Ghana, I saw the beauty of life and realised that perseverance and honesty is always key. I worked with street children teaching drama and English and knew I would return to the UK to teach. Drama is by far the most healing tool in the world, it can unite, educate and entertain all at once – drama is my first love and I owe a lot to this art form for helping me heal from so much.

On my return from Ghana, I went on to study a masters. I love learning but not necessarily writing essays. Education has been a vehicle in which I've been able to legally drive. It's opened doors for me that may have otherwise been closed. I have taught drama in many capacities, I absolutely love teaching, but have found the most joy running my first business Motivate Me Tutor working as a one to one English and drama tutor, choosing my own hours but also changing the lives of young people. In the last eight years I've worked with young people from many different backgrounds and always use holistic methods to motivate and inspire my students – and I'm so excited to be expanding and growing a team of tutors. My vision is big for this business, I want to inspire lots of young people but also allow young people to reach their potential regardless of their background. We moved mostly online two years ago, which has given me access to the whole world and made my business more accessible and able to work around my family.

My second business was a dream of mine for so long that I sometimes have to pinch myself that such a beautiful opportunity presented itself at the right time. I started researching routes into the travel industry in 2015. Initially I edged towards teaching travel and tourism, which was the safe option! My research continued and I investigated several travel franchises and embarked on finding a business coach at my local business centre to help with my business plan and secure funding. Then I discovered I was pregnant with my second child. I was a little shell-shocked and again that feeling of shame washed over me. I was pretty much a single mother and would now be a single mother with two children – still trying to create that legacy. Being a mother has challenged me. However, it's also given me so much joy, and the unconditional love that I have for my two babies is unreal and makes up for all the tough times. In November 2017, I gave birth to my beautiful daughter who, just like my son, has taught me so much about myself and the type of life I want for my family.

I thank God that they have brought a new sort of joy to my life.

I honestly believe dreams do come true. When my daughter was eight weeks old, I said yes to joining the Holiday Fixer as a self-employed travel consultant – crazy timing, I hear you say, but when you know something is for you, you just know. It's been the most thrilling decision of my entrepreneurial journey. It's been a whirlwind of learning, balancing the kids and the businesses, but you know I wouldn't change it. I'm always learning, evolving and embracing life.

No matter what your obstacles may be, take your

goals and break them down; each day is a new day and you really can achieve anything. People will sometimes make your dreams seem silly but remember it's your dream and not theirs.

Never ever lose sight of your vision; even when it seems impossible, keep striving for that vision and believe you have it already. I'm a long way from achieving my big goals, but I absolutely believe I can achieve anything. Losing my sight was traumatic but it has given me the drive to succeed and overcome adversity.

Running two businesses has not only provided me with the freedom to pick my own hours and work towards my dream of a legacy and financial freedom, but also has provided me with the opportunity to chase my dreams and raise my kids. I would be lying if I said it's always a walk in the park; it really isn't and the process is still a work in progress. I suffer from mum guilt all the time: Am I working too much? Am I not working enough? The lockdown really did put lots of things into perspective for me, that sometimes you have to say no and set realistic boundaries, set goals and outsource some of that workload. You can only do so much. Always do your best and never lose sight of your vision – you can do this! ♡

★★★

You can find Anita here:

http://theholidayfixer.com/

https://www.facebook.com/Anitatheholidayfixer/

Motivate Me Tutors
https://www.facebook.com/Motivate-me-Tutors-517453648779686/

# Series of Events!
## Becky Kennedy

*I would like to say a special thanks to my children, my family, my best friends and my partner, Dale, who has shown me what love should be and how happy life can be with the right person.*

Let me set the scene. It was the back end of 2017, it was a Sunday morning and an argument erupted. To be fair, it was not out of the blue; many things hadn't been going right in my relationship for a while – feeling alone, hours away from friends and family, feeling like a single parent doing it on my own – but as a mum you do what you think is best for the kids. If you stay in the situation even though you're unhappy, as a mum to two little ones under the age of four, the mum and dad should be together, right?

Well, it appears I couldn't have been more wrong! I was left sitting wondering what the hell had just happened, tears streaming down my face. What the hell was I going to do now? I certainly hadn't planned on being a single parent again, and homeless. I already had two older children from a previous failed relationship, but that's a whole other story!

Frustrated and left alone with the kids, I called my mum, all while continuing to wait for a glimmer of hope that this was just a bad argument and all would be well. But by that evening nothing, nada, zip, so I got the kids in the car along with a few belongings and drove the four and a half hours back to Manchester. Wow, what a drive that was: rain, sleet, snow storms and still confused by the day's events. But I got there at 1am and broke down, literally in a heap on the floor.

Now let's face it, anyone who has gone through a break up will probably admit you go through the stages of questioning yourself. What did I do wrong? Was there someone else? How could I make this better? Why did he not love me? How could this happen two weeks before Christmas? What about the kids, how will they deal with it? How will I manage? How will I cope? Where will we live? These questions go round and round until you drive yourself crazy; well, I know they did me.

I swore after the first relationship I was in when I was younger never to let myself get hurt again! I wonder how many of us have said that. I remember feeling such a dick! An utter fool thinking a happy ever after existed and I was worthy of the lifestyle I so longed for in my head for me and the kids, and oh my God, what would people say. Told you so, all happened too quickly, was never going to last – you know, the ones who are always there to stick the knife in at the opportune moment.

I remember sitting there two weeks after the event, in between Christmas and New Year, in my car alone, crying, questions going round and round in my head, one of them actually being *if I drove into that wall right now, would it be that bad?* Why does my life never seem to go right? Then there was a revelation that cleared up many questions I had, which stopped me questioning myself and instead got me thinking *how do I do this alone?* Was I scared? You have no fucking idea!

After sleeping on floors, blow up beds, sofas at family and friends with the kids for nearly five months, I got the call… 'Miss Kennedy, we are pleased to offer you a house'! My response, "Really, this isn't a wind up?" The tears flowed again but this time of joy. At last, something had gone right. Was the house where I wanted it to be? No, but we had a house. Now I could start to rebuild our lives and be the best mum I could be… Plus, to be honest, I wasn't sure how much more my back could take!

So, the day arrived for me to get the keys to the house. I remember being so excited, like a kid at Christmas. All I can say is thank God for my best friend Natalie. She saved me from despair. For seventy-two hours non-stop, all we did was clean. I swear to God, we smelled like we had both bathed in bleach! I'm sitting here now writing this smiling because honestly what a three days that was. Looking back, we can laugh at the time we made the air blue with the choice of words we used, let me tell you! If you had seen the house the council had given me – don't get me wrong, I was grateful, so very grateful for the house, for the fresh start – but bleaching even the walls and floorboards had not been part of my master plan on how to rebuild my life. Nor hers, I don't believe! But she was a trooper and just as OCD as me, so we smashed it together.

So, after an eventful few days, we managed to get us in the house, still not feeling 100%. You know the days you have with those 'how am I going to do this' moments, no money in the bank, a whole house to decorate, furniture to buy, no carpets and a broken bed… OMG the bed! After realising the middle leg was missing while trying to build it, my best friend Sarah, who to be fair is more like a sister, and I had to come up with plan B, which consisted of grabbing a boulder from the garden, giving it a wash and propping the bed up!

We all need carpets, especially when the alternative is bare floorboards, so I called the carpet company, appointment booked and quote received, and nope that wasn't happening at that price! So plan B – thank God for plan B – was to get the cheapest carpets in only the rooms where they were essential and fit them myself armed with a Stanley knife and a roll of cord carpet, which I picked up in my car. You should have seen the guys at the carpet place, they must have thought I was a right nutter, but I set to work after my dad showed me the right way to cut it… who knew there was a right way? I soon learnt.

But something had to give. I felt like the weight of the world was on my shoulders: how to be a good mum, how to be Becky again, how to provide for the kids, how to pay the bills, how to pay the debt from being with my ex-partner, it just all seemed never ending. I mean, we are not a fancy family or anything but these are basic essential items we needed. I felt like the world's biggest failure. It started to seem like I spent more nights crying in the shower than I did out of it, just so the kids couldn't hear me or see me this way.

Don't get me wrong, I looked into going back to work. I had spent years in Credit Control, I loved it and had been good at it, but with two kids under four, childcare isn't cheap. The hours I would have to work to even cover costs literally meant I would be working for a £1 an hour but losing all the special moments with the kids. I remember thinking *Jesus, give me a break!* Why is being a mum sometimes a constant battle between your head and your heart, what you want to do for your kids and what you can do?

They say you can't have it all and as much as I wanted to work as I always had, I wanted to spend time with my kids, you see, at the same time as trying to get our lives back on track, sort the house and maybe even remember who the fuck I was before feeling like a worthless human being.

My son was going through assessments for autism; a whole new can of worms now just opened up. You look for someone to blame, you question *why my son, how has this happened, what did I do wrong*? The worst part is you will never get answers to these questions and, to be honest, two years later, looking back, I find the questions never mattered. You go round in circles being consumed in guilt, it somehow being your fault. But what I found really mattered was getting the right people involved, asking for and seeking the help, learning as much as you can about autism. Honestly, I'm still learning now about autism and finding ways to help my son on good and bad days.

Then there were the appointments. It was unreal. Every other week was a new appointment letter on the doorstep. So back to the looking for a job… I mean, who was going to hire me then give me five or six days a month off for the paediatrician, dietician, speech and language, education office via the nursery he attended, sign language classes? It seemed never ending, but he was my priority and so was getting the diagnosis, so I could move forward and help him the best I could.

So back to the drawing board. I had been involved with network marketing before as a hobby. It intrigued me. It showed me you could make money from home round your kids and commitments but it also showed me that you can do a lot of work for not a lot of money. As with any industry, there is good and bad! I spent that summer partnered with a company I liked, but I wasn't passionate about. It didn't provide me with that buzz or excitement or with the help or support I needed. I was just a number, a sales statistic unless ordering like a machine, I wasn't really part of anything. I didn't make any real money in that company but what it did do was help me build my profile online and make friends. It also showed me what I didn't like about the industry and opened my eyes to how it should be done.

By now it was August 2018 and I was ready to give up. How much longer can you try? It is fucking tiring constantly feeing like you're battling to live – no, scrap that, survive! Then a message popped up in my inbox from a lady called Katie. We had been friends for a while on Facebook but never really spoke. She was asking how I was, she seemed excited and I asked why.

Katie then told me about a brand new company opening the next month: Krizma Cosmetics. It was an idea thought of round a dining table by a lady she knew, Sam. Well, I have to admit curiosity got the better of me but I had that nagging feeling: could I really be arsed putting in effort to get no results? I was so done with the bullshit of network marketing, so I said I would think about it and I did for the next few days. But it played on my mind constantly. Could this be the company I had been looking for with the opportunity that could change my life? What did I have to lose? Surely it would be worth a go at least?

After another conversation with Katie, I joined up and registered, and wow what a whirlwind! Not only was it a crazy busy time being the run up to Christmas but suddenly people were joining me, little old me. I'd never had a team before and suddenly I had thirty-two women asking how to run their business and what Krizma was about!

I got invited to a meeting at the CEO's house with Katie. Overwhelmed was an understatement! I remember I don't think I spoke more than fifty words all night, I just listened and took it all in. On the drive home, something clicked in my head: in that moment I realised after sitting with Samantha Prendergast talking about this business that I had made the right decision. The company was built on inspiring, empowering, supporting others, BOOM! Exactly what I hadn't found yet. Now, don't get me wrong, other companies out there work well for many reasons, my point is you have to find the company that gives you that lightbulb moment, the right company for you!

By November 2018, momentum was growing and I started to believe more in myself. When people say you have to surround yourself with others who inspire you, they aren't wrong. Previously, I was in the mindset of 'I can't do this', which had come from years of trying. But what I have come to realise is you should never stop trying, you just have to make sure when you're trying you have the right people around you.

Suddenly here I was, part of an opportunity that I could do, after many conversations with Katie and Sam (there was some belters, let me tell you, they must have thought *Jesus, this woman and her questions*) but it happened. I started to believe in myself again, my confidence started creeping back and it was like a new lease of life after feeling worthless for so long. I finally started to see glimpses of Becky, the one who had dreams, the one with the can-do attitude, the one who doesn't give up because it isn't in her nature!

That same month, Sam decided to do a 'free to join' and the team jumped to over 170 in a week. I had my days of feeling lost, I mean could I really do this, help others, grow a team, spend more time with my kids, balance out work and home, earn an income and not have to keep checking and worrying about bills?

Those thoughts now seem like a lifetime ago. The whole thing has been a learning curve. I have now been with the company twenty-three months, my team is over 430 strong ladies and gents all achieving as one team together, I hold regular trainings, meetings, I helped with ideas for the compensation plan, and the team hit £500,000 sales in just ten months from September 2019 to June 2020 – say what?! The best part is that we have done it as a team.

Never in a million years if you had asked me in December 2017 would I have thought this to be my life, I just decided to go for it! Have I achieved my end goal? Hell no! Will I stop until I have? Not a chance! Never give up on your dreams. Life can change in a heartbeat and I want others to see life can throw you curveballs, some big, some small, but you have the ability to overcome them. Believe in yourself and you will become the person you know you're capable of being!

★★★

You can find Becky here:

Website: becky-kennedy.com
Facebook:
https://www.facebook.com/becky.kennedy.12327

# Your Life, Your Responsibility

## Carla Maria

*I want to thank my family and friends for your continuous love and support, despite not always understanding what I do and why!*
*A special mention to my bestie Brogan. You are my absolute rock!!! You are one of the few people I can count on through the good times and the bad, and are quite possibly the only person who thinks I haven't gone crazy at some point lol! Your love, support and encouragement mean the world to me – thank you for being you.*

Have you ever looked around you and thought, "Everything I have or don't have is because of me. I have created this exact version of my life."

Let that just sink in for a couple of seconds… every single thing you have or don't have is because of YOU!!!!

How does that make you feel? Does it make you feel slightly uneasy? Has it made you feel a tad defensive?

Excellent – that was my intention!! (In a nice way, of course!)

Hearing the truth can sting a little, and if it didn't

stir some emotions inside of you, you either have everything you want in life, or you're quite frankly in denial!

Now your instant reaction to all of this might be to get defensive, and tell me I'm wrong… and that's okay, I used to think that way too!

But just so you know, I'm not wrong!

Trust me when I say that not long ago, I used to be where you are now, and I get you, I really do! This is why I want to help you! Personal responsibility isn't something that's talked about much, but it's something that drives the direction of our lives, something that if ignored has the ability to let us live a life we're not truly happy with.

My intention for writing this chapter is to help you see what's possible, to help you break free from the ties that are holding you back, and to allow you to become free! The best thing you can ever do for yourself is to take 100% responsibility for every single thing in your life – the good, the bad and the ugly!!

## Quit the Blame Game

Throughout our lives, we can become that conditioned to thinking and feeling a certain way that often it's beyond us to even imagine other possibilities. We get caught up playing the blame game – you know the one, where something goes wrong in our lives and we instantly have to find someone or something at fault. Because God forbid it could actually be us at fault!! That's just not possible – or is it??

Whilst assigning blame to every Tom, Dick and Harry may seem like the easiest way to excuse our undesirable outcomes, it will lead you nowhere pretty fast. When something goes wrong, or we don't get what we want, we instantly try and find fault. Problem being that we don't look closely enough to home to find the real cause. When you stop putting the blame on others for your undesired outcomes and start looking at the actual cause, only then can you even begin to start moving forward. We've all been there, some more than others, some are still there, some have managed to pull themselves out – but know that you are not alone!

And yes, I hear you, it's easier said than done!! I know that, believe me! I used to go through life and make decisions, be it conscious or unconscious, which sometimes led to results I didn't want. But instead of owning my decisions, I did what felt like the most natural thing to do – I blamed anyone and everything in sight. Everyone excluding me, of course!

Let me put this into context for you. A couple of years ago, I wanted to start my own fitness brand. I had everything ready, leggings and tops all designed and made, website, social media accounts, the lot – I was pretty much set! However, there was one major problem: when the leggings arrived, every single pair was see-through, which definitely was not the look I was going for!! To say I was distraught was an understatement. I couldn't think of the situation without wanting to cry.

And my first reaction was to find fault, who was to blame for this? Why has this happened so close to launch? Why me? The usual. Now after a few months had passed and I was finally able to reflect without having a complete meltdown, I realised this happened because of me. Because there were things I did, and more importantly because there were things I didn't do. It was a very costly lesson but one I wouldn't change now for the world, as it forced me to see things differently and it forced me to admit fault and grow.

## Get Rid of All the BS Excuses

In order to take full responsibility of your results, you need to ditch the excuses, all of them! I know you love them, I did too – they make you feel so much better about yourself, don't they?! Why would you need to take personal responsibility when you've got perfectly valid excuses to fall back on? However, when you think about it, they are literally just that, excuses! Excuses cloud your judgement; they lead you down a false path of security and allow you to hide.

In November 2018, some of my excuses got put to the test. For years I had wanted to do a bikini competition after whipping my body into shape doing Crossfit in Australia in 2013. But I used every excuse I could think of not to do it – I didn't have a coach, I didn't know where to find a coach, I love my food too much to diet, could I actually reach that level, it's too much commitment – all perfectly valid reasons to not do it; well, that's what I told myself, anyway. But I was put to the test when my personal trainer said he would be my coach. Instant reaction was "F★ck"! I had nothing to hide behind now! All my perfectly valid excuses blown out of the water in one sentence!

Was it easy? Hell no, there were times I wanted to cry like a little girl and quit! But I knew I was stronger than that, and more importantly my desire to hit the stage had grown way beyond any excuse! So, in September 2019, after months of training and dieting, I hit the stage at the UKBFF championships in Belfast where I walked away with first place! First f★cking place!! Five years I had let my excuses hold me back, and for what?? Trouble is, I didn't even realise I was allowing these excuses to dictate what I wanted. And that's the problem with excuses, they're crafty and are excellent at providing you with that false alibi you need to justify whatever it is you are/are not doing.

So, let me ask you, what excuses are you using that are holding you back from doing what you want in life?

"I'm too tired to go to the gym."

"I don't know where to start."

"I don't have the money."

"I don't have the time."

"I don't have the skills/qualifications."

I have used all of these excuses and hundreds more throughout my lifetime. But excuses never got me the results I wanted. Excuses meant not facing my fears, it meant I didn't deal with issues that needed dealing with and they also meant never pushing myself far enough out of my comfort zone to see any real difference.

When you call yourself out on your BS you start to make better choices; try it and see what happens!

OWN YOUR DECISIONS

We all have situations in life where we are presented with a decision, something that forces us to make a choice. Sometimes we make the right decision and get a result we like, but other times we make the wrong one and end up with something we'd rather not have.

Now before we go any further, I just want you to know that it's okay to make the wrong choice, we're human and it's what we do! We can't get it right all of the time, the key is to get it right the majority of the time!

The fact that none of us are perfect means every so often we mess up and get it wrong. The easiest and best way is to own that wrong decision, fix it and move forward. But at times that means short-term pain, and we tend to want to stay away from pain at all costs. Even at the cost of our health and happiness.

Here's an example of where I've been and where I have seen so many people:

You're in a relationship that you know you no longer want to be in. It's toxic, it's making you unhappy, you want out, yet you're still there. Now YOU have two options here, either stay in the relationship or end it and move on. Staying will cause more unhappiness and may even have an impact on your mental health. Leaving will temporarily cause pain, you'll be adjusting to being single, you start doubting if you want to be single, you start doubting your decision along the lines of "it's not all bad, he's nice sometimes", etc., etc. This will pass and you'll come out of the other end wondering why on earth you stayed as long as you did!

Now whether you decide to stay in this relationship or leave, know that the choice is yours! And I'm going to get really honest here, you have to live with the consequences of that decision. How can you complain about something that makes you so unhappy, that you have the ability to change – but don't!

Now that's a super obvious one but what about those little daily choices we make that seem really insignificant? These are just as bad, as over time they compound and can end up having a huge effect on you.

Ever feel that one wee slip up in your healthy eating isn't an issue, which by the way it isn't if that's all it is? But who's been in the position where one slip up led to two, then three – then next thing the diet's out of the window and you're back to telling yourself that dieting is hard, that you're not able to eat well, good food is expensive – all the BS to justify your choice.

Or your credit cards, sneaky wee f*ckers, them! One day you're loving life with all this "extra" money, not even thinking about having to pay things back. Then one day you wake up and the frigging thing's maxed out – like, how and when the hell did that actually happen?! I'll tell you exactly how, by making that choice every single time you used it, even though it meant having it all to pay back!

Every single decision you make, be it small or large, has the ability to have a positive or negative impact on your life. The choice is yours, and you have to own that!

## Victim Or Victor

Now, I just want to clarify here, what I mean by victim is having a victim mentality. You know the one, when it feels that everything bad is happening to you, woe is me type thing, where you've somehow managed to get a major chip on your shoulder, thinking the world owes you a favour.

NO! You need to recognise and get out of this mentality ASAP! As amazing as you think you are – and yes, I agree with you, you are – you simply cannot progress in life if you're playing the victim.

A person with a victim mindset takes NO RESPONSIBILITY for the events in their lives. Like none, zero, zilch, nada. They get consumed with experiences from the past and are constantly repeating negative thought patterns wondering why things never change. They effortlessly find the negatives in every situation and use their own situation to their advantage by gaining sympathy from others. But it's not easy being a victim, and the biggest challenge that a person with a victim mindset faces is their resistance to change. Things are very much black or white in their eyes and to see things differently may mean having to take some form of personal responsibility, and accept that changes have to be made. This is an extremely hard pill to swallow but in order to get out of your own way, you must acknowledge the victim mindset and become the victor!

I say this to people all the time, if you don't like it change it! Something I was faced with when it came to making the decision to leave the police service of Northern Ireland. Whilst I made some class friends, friends I will have for life, I wasn't happy. I didn't see myself spending the next thirty-odd years as a police officer, so I made the decision to resign.

Was it an easy one? Most definitely not! I toyed with the idea on and off for about three years! But in the end, I'd had enough. Enough of being unhappy, enough of having my life controlled by people I didn't even know, but more importantly I'd had enough of playing the victim – I was done!

When I thought about it, it all came down to the following:

Who picked this job? Me.

Who was letting people I didn't know control my life? Me again!

Who was the one deciding to stay despite being unhappy? That would be me, again!

Who was the one complaining flat out but was doing nothing about it? Yep, you guessed it, me!

See the recurring theme there?

I could have continued the rest of my days in that job quite easily as I was good at it but in the end I realised that it was me, and only me, that can make me happy. And if that meant leaving this well-paid job, then so be it. So, I did, and I can hand-on-heart say I haven't missed that job one day since I drove out of the station gates on Sunday 16th September 2012!

I just want you to know that you ALWAYS have a choice. Yes at times it will be difficult, but don't let outside circumstances control the way you think, feel and act. Know that your life is 100% YOUR responsibility!!!! No-one or no thing can dictate what direction your life goes in unless you allow it, it's that simple!! Sometimes things go to plan, sometimes they don't. Sometimes you get what you want, sometimes you don't. But by taking control of your actions you take control of your results. And if you don't like the results you're getting, then change what it is you are doing. Rinse and repeat until finally one day that life you're craving right now will be yours!

★★★

You can find Carla here:

> https://www.facebook.com/carla.maria.1420

# The Gardener and the Flower

## Casey Bird

*To the soulmate that has shared the last eleven years with me, you have been my rock, with me through everything. Your kindness cannot be matched. You supported and encouraged me to chase my dreams and choose myself, knowing it was the best decision for my life. You were the gardener to my flower, and you let me bloom. This decision has meant a heart-wrenching change for us. But I know you watch on and can see I am becoming who I was truly meant to be. You will remain with me always. Love, your Bird.*

It was the last hug, the last kiss. It should have lingered longer but the chauffeur was standing waiting impatiently for me to get into the car, so I felt rushed. Tears were beginning to roll down my cheeks and I was about to completely lose it before he said, 'It's going to be okay, everything is going to be okay, this is just the next chapter in our story and our story has a very happy ending.' So, with that reassurance, I jumped in the back of the car and was on my way to take what was to be one of my final flights home to Australia.

I had chosen me; I had chosen this path. I knew it was time to put me first.

How did I get to that heart-wrenching moment? For years I had been compromising quite happily – but not really knowing I was, if that makes sense. I was living what I thought life was supposed to be. I had moved to another country to be with an amazing man and started living a life there with a decent job that paid the bills. I was in love, we were going on holidays and vacations, eating out a lot (which I love to do – I'm all about the food) and doing day-to-day things you think are what life is meant to be about. But one day I started feeling restless, irritated and my mind started to wonder and believe that there had to be more to this life than a decent job and a holiday once a year.

The years were passing by so quickly and I was spending longer and longer away from my family and oldest friends. I started to become resentful of the compromises I was making. Yes, I had made the choices to be where I was, but those choices were no longer serving my soul and I was losing who I was. I had forgotten what I truly needed to feel satisfied and happy in life. I wanted to live a bigger, more fulfilled life for my soul. You see, even though I was in love and living what seemed a great life, inside I felt there was something else I needed, a piece was missing. It wasn't anyone's fault, I realise now, and have come to learn that I needed to make myself happy.

You cannot make a person happy; it wasn't anyone's responsibility to make me happy. You can make a person smile, you can make them feel good, you can make them laugh, but whether or not a person is happy is out of your control. I realised I wasn't completely happy, and I needed to take a journey to get that back no matter what. I had to choose me.

Maybe some of you are thinking my life didn't sound that bad, I should have been grateful for what I had. And yes, to anyone on the outside looking in, it may certainly have looked that way. I was in love, I was doing things I loved, but inside there was still something that I needed, and I think that was a sense of purpose. I had to start making choices that truly aligned with what I was craving in life. I feel like as women we are capable of having so much, to be more, live more, but we settle (well, not all of us, but a lot of us). I didn't want to settle on any aspect of my life, and I knew I had to make more choices to force me to change my current circumstances. And now I look back, I probably waited too long to make them. But hey, we live and learn.

I think everyone in this life has different callings and mine was just a bigger calling than the life I was living. I wanted it all. I needed a purpose in life, I want to serve and help others, I wanted to be financially independent and self-sufficient, I wanted to holiday to many places, at many times of the year, I wanted the option to have babies, if I chose, I wanted love and to share all of this with my person. Most of all, I wanted to be undeniably happy.

I'm a big dreamer, a believer that I can have it all, and I have a real issue with someone telling me I can't have it or do it all. Just try and tell me no, I won't have it! I just got to a point where if I didn't start living the way I was being called to live, I was going to live half a life – I wanted to live fully. So that then leads me to how I began to make choices that started to align with my true purpose in life. Where did I even start? What was it that I wanted?

I suppose it started with the decision that I needed to make a decision! *Just make a decision already*, I told myself! So, instead of procrastinating, and let me tell you I was the world's biggest procrastinator, I just decided.

The first decision I made was starting something new, a business venture. I had many ideas about businesses I wanted to start, which I'll touch on later, but this was my first stepping stone and this one has had the most impact on my life, has given me further choices and flexibility in life and allowed me to truly become the woman I always knew was inside of me.

You see, those who know me will understand this and agree, I was never one for working for someone else. I struggled with being told what to do and when to do it (I can see my friends all nodding along, in total agreement to this). I was just lucky that I had very understanding bosses along my journey that allowed me to 'somewhat' spread my wings and work more independently at what I was doing for them. And for a while it worked well, but eventually I became restless and I felt the same old pull to do something more, and I wanted out. Becoming my own boss has been the best decision I've made.

Now, in saying that, it wasn't like I made this great

decision and things all just worked out peachy straight away. I have to be real with you, being your own boss takes a lot of personal development and mindset work. It takes dedication, consistency and effort. And I found this out really early when I wasn't experiencing the kind of success I dreamt about. And yes, I wondered if I had in fact made the right decision at all. Why could I see others who had made the same choice I did succeed, and I wasn't succeeding, what was their secret?

I later found out the key difference is that they worked on themselves every day. They opened themselves up to other ways of learning, growing and developing, and they did it consistently. They were in a positive mindset, a mindset of trust and belief in themselves. They also had direction and did things differently. I always pushed away working on myself, the personal development that everyone always said was key to success. I don't know why, I just didn't understand it, maybe thought I'd be wasting my time. Well, let me tell you, I was soooo wrong about this. Yes, I know it's easy for me to just say 'change your mindset' or 'read a personal development book', but you definitely do have to be open and ready to do this. I was sick of not seeing results I wanted, so I was ready to try anything at that point and to choose to invest in me.

So, to start my personal development journey I started to read. I could never be bothered with reading, I'd always start and never finish a book. I just got bored. But I started with the aim to finish just one book. And so it began. I finished one book and picked up another and I kept it up. Go me!

I also invested in an online academy that was referred to me from a friend, and as soon as I began that academy it was like a lightbulb went on in my brain. This, my friends, was the exact turning point for me. The academy taught me all the practical skills I needed as well as opening me up to a different way of thinking. They completely changed my mindset and how I talked to myself and others, and how I feel about myself. This piece was HUGE for me because for so long I was so negative towards myself, not realising the detrimental effect that actually has on us as humans.

Once I made that decision to invest in that academy things changed. I had direction and clarity on my business, where I was going and how to get there. I became so confident in how I was showing up for myself and, because of that, I became this calm, kind, more positive person. It sounds weird, but I feel like I was so erratic before, I was frustrated and angry and I wasn't putting my best self forward in any aspect in life and that wasn't good for anyone. I WAS STUCK.

The decision to choose me and invest in this academy made EVERYTHING start to fall into place for me. It didn't happen overnight, but it was happening. I was just taking small steps, implementing what I had learnt. I was showing up in a different way, my energy was attracting great things and I started to let go of the negative feelings of resentment, anger and the frustration I was constantly feeling for as long as I could remember. I could finally see a light and a bright future.

This is why I am so passionate about finding your

purpose and choosing you. Because when you do, you show up as the person you're meant to be, the best version of you. Unfortunately, I wasn't living my true purpose for a long time and that had a detrimental effect on my relationship and ultimately led me to move home to find myself. Like I said, you have to make yourself happy first, you cannot place the responsibility on someone else to do this for you. Putting someone in a position where they have to constantly fill up someone else's cup leads to anger, frustration and ultimately you break apart from people. I didn't want that, so I had to start my journey to make myself fully happy.

I heard a beautiful saying recently about the gardener/flower theory – the gardener wants to tend to the flower, to allow it to become what it was truly designed to be. The gardener doesn't demand it to become a different flower, a flower he wants it to be for his ego. He just wants the flower to bloom the ways it's meant to. Being happy is allowing yourself or someone to be who they are truly designed to be, not what others expect you to be.

I needed to become who I was truly designed to be.

Once my feet hit home soil it was like the floodgates of abundance opened with full force. I truly believe my decision sent a massive signal to the universe that I was ready for change. Within six months I promoted up two levels in my online business, receiving bonuses and recognition along the way. I had opened, and was successfully running a business that I had dreamt about for a long time, an infrared sauna business from home.

I have a massive passion for health and finding ways to heal ourselves, so this was an exciting time to unveil this venture to the world.

I had also connected and reconnected with friends who totally got where I was heading in life and were so supportive and wanted to come along for the ride. But what I was most proud of is that I was beginning to stand on my own two feet (sort of) and I felt a sense of purpose, FINALLY that I was doing 'the things' I was designed to do. Obviously, I have so much more to achieve, but I'm still growing and learning, and I'm miles ahead of where I thought I would be. I will always thank the person who referred me to the women who helped me on my transformation journey and who continue to help me transform daily. They know who they are.

When I sat down to start writing this chapter, I was afraid my message would get lost; I hope it doesn't. My hope is that you see that even though I was living what seemed to be a great life and I had great love, a house and supportive friends, my soul wasn't fulfilled. This wasn't about anyone else, this journey is about me and is one I'm taking to find myself again. I had to listen to my calling to do something more with my life. I chose me. I chose to make myself happy, knowing what I could lose.

It was the hardest decision I'll ever make, and it meant I lost something that is incredibly important to me, a partner, a bestie, a support system that was so dear to me. Someone who I wanted to share this new life with, this newer version of me with. It meant heartache like I've never felt before. Although I lost this part of my purpose and choosing you. Because when you do, you show up as the person you're meant to be, the best version of you. Unfortunately, I wasn't living my true purpose for a long time and that had a detrimental effect on my relationship and ultimately led me to move home to find myself. Like I said, you have to make yourself happy first, you cannot place the responsibility on someone else to do this for you. Putting someone in a position where they have to constantly fill up someone else's cup leads to anger, frustration and ultimately you break apart from people. I didn't want that, so I had to start my journey to make myself fully happy.

I heard a beautiful saying recently about the gardener/flower theory – the gardener wants to tend to the flower, to allow it to become what it was truly designed to be. The gardener doesn't demand it to become a different flower, a flower he wants it to be for his ego. He just wants the flower to bloom the ways it's meant to. Being happy is allowing yourself or someone to be who they are truly designed to be, not what others expect you to be.

I needed to become who I was truly designed to be.

Once my feet hit home soil it was like the floodgates of abundance opened with full force. I truly believe my decision sent a massive signal to the universe that I was ready for change. Within six months I promoted up two levels in my online business, receiving bonuses and recognition along the way. I had opened, and was successfully running a business that I had dreamt about for a long time, an infrared sauna business from home.

I have a massive passion for health and finding ways to heal ourselves, so this was an exciting time to unveil this venture to the world.

I had also connected and reconnected with friends who totally got where I was heading in life and were so supportive and wanted to come along for the ride. But what I was most proud of is that I was beginning to stand on my own two feet (sort of) and I felt a sense of purpose, FINALLY that I was doing 'the things' I was designed to do. Obviously, I have so much more to achieve, but I'm still growing and learning, and I'm miles ahead of where I thought I would be. I will always thank the person who referred me to the women who helped me on my transformation journey and who continue to help me transform daily. They know who they are.

When I sat down to start writing this chapter, I was afraid my message would get lost; I hope it doesn't. My hope is that you see that even though I was living what seemed to be a great life and I had great love, a house and supportive friends, my soul wasn't fulfilled. This wasn't about anyone else, this journey is about me and is one I'm taking to find myself again. I had to listen to my calling to do something more with my life. I chose me. I chose to make myself happy, knowing what I could lose.

It was the hardest decision I'll ever make, and it meant I lost something that is incredibly important to me, a partner, a bestie, a support system that was so dear to me. Someone who I wanted to share this new life with, this newer version of me with. It meant heartache like I've never felt before. Although I lost this part of my life, I still hold hope we will reconnect one day (because I dare to dream). I still have so much love for him, and he is one of my biggest supporters.

The right decisions are always the hardest to make. But they must be made in order to live the life we deserve. Yes, the choices I made led to gut-wrenching heartache, but they have also led me to feel a great sense of purpose, where I am seeing so much abundance. I am around family and friends daily, I have new friendships and business partnerships, which are forming and growing and I finally have a sense that I am living my soul's true purpose.

I am finally choosing me and giving myself permission to be happy. I know once I am truly happy, I will thrive in all relationships, never placing responsibility on someone to fill my cup. I will be the best version of myself, bringing my very best to all relationships in life. Choose you – always.

★★★

You can find Casey here:

> https://linktr.ee/the_birdie_diaries

# You Control Your Future
## Claire Maynard

*I am dedicating this chapter to my past self, in recognition and gratitude for keeping going, taking back control, staying strong, dreaming big and never giving up. Because if I hadn't have done that I wouldn't be where I am today. I'm also dedicating it to you and other women who are determined to build a better life for themselves and their families no matter what their past or present reality is, to be true to themselves and continue to rise.*

I thought the best way to start this chapter would be to start from my lowest point and work outwards. But when I sat down to write, I realised that this would be genuinely hard for me as I've had many very low points, which to me were equally as low in different ways. Points in my life where I thought things couldn't get any worse, points when things happened that I thought I couldn't come back from. If I could paint an overall picture it would be of a girl and then woman who completely lost sight of and connection with herself. Someone who spent the whole of their twenties and half of their thirties trying to fill a hole they didn't know existed.

Someone with low self-esteem, little confidence, who felt completely lost in the world, and who wanted more from life but didn't know how to get it or where to start.

But this isn't a story of tragedy or desperation, it's one of courage, grit and determination. I share my story to show you that our past and even our present doesn't have to define our future. That your current reality doesn't have to be how your whole life plays out, anyone can change their life if they really want to, no matter what their circumstances. I want to help to inspire and empower you to fight for a better life for you and your family, to break out of the rut and leave the mundane behind.

At the age of twenty-four my dad took his own life; the shock, loss and grief were crippling. I felt even more lost than I had before, the grief was overwhelming, and the unanswered questions were almost too much to bear. Why had he done it? Why hadn't I seen it coming? Why wasn't I enough? Did he not love me? Could I have stopped it? I barely ate, I barely slept and felt like my feet weren't even touching the ground. The responsibility of organising the funeral and all of the arrangements put even more pressure on my already fragile mental health. It was like I'd taken on his pain and had no outlet for it. But I did it, I survived it, I learned how to adjust and how to carry on. I lived with the pain and turmoil for a long time, but then I decided I had to let it go. This was not what he would have wanted for me, this is not what I wanted for me. I had no control over what he did, but I could control how I responded and how I moved forward in my life.

That point about control is an important one. I did a spider diagram to help me write this chapter and a recurring theme throughout all the past events that help make up my story was control, or more to the point, lack of it. Things that have been out of my control in one way or another; mental illness, loss/death, addiction, someone taking my control, chronic illness, bullying. We cannot control these things, but we can control our response to it and when we do, that is when we become truly empowered and unstoppable women. I'm going to give you some examples of this from my own story.

When my anxiety first started, I was sitting in a caravan with my one year old, wondering where we were going to live and what I was going to do. My life as I knew it was ripped out from under my feet, the uncertainty and responsibility weighing down hard. I used to lie awake at night with this sick feeling in the pit of my stomach, feeling my heart pounding out of my chest. The slightest thing would bring on an overwhelming feeling of panic and worry. I felt everything crumbling around me, again, with no idea how to pull through. Yet again a symptom of loss of control, I needed to find a way to take my power back, and I did. It wasn't easy and it took time, but I did it. I looked to the future, to what I wanted for my life and my daughter's life, I made a plan and I got to work. Now life being what it is, that plan didn't work out, but it set me on a whole different path, an even better one!

However, there were more bumps in the road to come and I didn't see this one coming either. I don't know how long I'd had depression, but I remember the point when I realised that something was wrong. I was walking with my daughter by a stream and knew I should be enjoying the moment, treasuring it and smiling. But instead I felt detached, disassociated, like I was floating above my body watching what was going on rather than living it. I felt no emotion, no joy, the complete opposite of the months I had suffered with anxiety. I was constantly exhausted, deflated and flat. It was like I was on a treadmill; eat, sleep, work, repeat, floating through life just existing and not actually LIVING. I'm sure it didn't help that I was in a job I hated and never had any money to actually do anything or give my daughter the experiences I wanted to, but I'm not sure how or when it started.

The same can be said for my addiction. In many ways, addiction is like depression, you can't pinpoint when it starts, only when you realise you have it. It's like you're living in your own bubble, without seeing the bigger picture or ripple effect on your life or the outside world. You live day to day frantically trying to regain something you don't even know you've lost. The more control you lose the harder it is to regain; it's like a negative downward spiral you can't stop. One day I woke up with a dry mouth, a headache and very little memory of the night before; I had blacked out, again. My anxiety was through the roof, I wanted to cry, I felt sick and I had no idea what had happened to the life I once knew. I was no longer in control of anything, my drinking, my mind, my mental health, my physical health or my life. I had no self-esteem, no confidence, no direction and no hope for the future. I was stuck in a rut, in a negative bubble with what felt like no way out of it. I knew things had to change or I would lose everything I had left, but I didn't know how.

This is when, completely by accident at first, my entrepreneurial journey began. I made a decision, a decision to take back control of my life, of everything. To live my life the way I wanted to and not how I was told I should, to leave the job I hated, to do things that set my heart and soul on fire, and to fight for the life I wanted for me and my daughter. I didn't know exactly how I was going to do it, just that I had to, as there was more to life than what I currently had. Now, don't get me wrong, it is easier said than done and has not been without its own challenges. But the skills I have learned along the way have not only helped me with my business, but also in processing and coming to terms with parts of my past and have helped me become who I am today. In fact, this journey has been my therapy. It's helped me to process past events and traumas, forgive, release and move forward. Throughout my business journey I have had to learn resilience, self-reflection, grit and determination. There have been let downs, frustrations, disappointment and what felt like mountains to climb. I had to try several different businesses before I found one that I was truly aligned to and passionate about. I've had rejections, and what seemed like failures, all of which have helped me get to where I am today. Business is much like life; to get the most out of it you must learn, grow and develop, you must learn not to take knocks personally and keep going no matter what. Keep remembering why you are doing it and what you want to get from it. You get out what you put in and you must not give up when things get tough. Once again it is about control; you cannot control what others think, do or say, or what external factors and events affect you or your business, but you can control how you respond, what you do about it, your own actions and your own thoughts.

After closing down one business and leaving another that I felt I wasn't aligned to, I was one month into my new (and current) business when I got the devastating news that I had a debilitating chronic illness. I had suspected things weren't right for a while and had been having extensive medical tests to get to the bottom of my symptoms. Now, although it was a relief to get a diagnosis, it was not one I wanted as it meant having to accept certain things about my present and future I did not want to. My first thoughts were, how can I build or run a business? How can I be successful? The answer, of course, was take back control! I couldn't control the fact that I had this illness, but I could control how I managed it, how I perceived myself and the thoughts and actions I took from that point forward. So, I learnt how to manage it, learnt how to schedule work around it, when to take a break, and to not work on a bad day. And in fact, having my own business is much better than being employed because I most likely would have had to leave a job, but my business is flexible, and I can work around my illness.

So how have I done this? How am I creating a freedom lifestyle where I am 100% present for my daughter, can work from anywhere in the world and in a few years will be completely financially free and living in abundance (as a single mum)? Well, I have done the inner work and personal development, worked on my confidence and self-esteem, I have learned the skills and strategies to build an online business (all of which are continuing, ongoing processes) with the help of people who have done it before me. I am a strong believer in women helping other women, that we are stronger and better together, and when we help each other amazing things happen. I have many mentors and friends within the online business industry who have helped me to develop both personally and professionally, so surround yourself with these types of people, people you can learn from and people who inspire you.

My message to you is: Don't let your past define you or dictate your future. You don't need to be wealthy or experienced to get out there and achieve your dreams or create the life you want. Anyone can change their life if they really want to. I have, and if I can, you can! If you want to be confident, empowered and determined, take back CONTROL. Fight for what you want and for a better future for you and your family, stay strong, don't listen to negativity and never give up on your dreams xxx

★★★

You can find Claire here:

https://linktr.ee/Clairemaynard

# Breaking Free from the Voices in Your Head

## Debbie Patrick

*This chapter is dedicated to my amazing children, Steven, Melissa, Hunter, Kayla, Hope and Sonny, without whom I might not be in this world today. It was having them that gave me the courage and drive to make it through the toughest times in our lives. Also, to any women out there that have allowed themselves to be abused, mentally or physically, told they were not good enough and believed it! To any women that have been alone and struggled to provide for their children. YOU are good enough, and you are capable of more than you know! BREAK FREE of what is holding you back, BELIEVE in yourself and you will ACHIEVE your dreams!*

I sat there in my tiny hotel room holding my six-month-old little boy trying to hold back the tears, unable to move as my little girls were playing on the floor beside me. I needed to move and move quickly as the hotel manager had just come and told me we had to leave and would be calling the police if I was not out in one hour. Because I was in an extremely volatile relationship and our home had become so unstable, my oldest children were living with their father. My parents were not speaking to me because I had continued to stay in the volatile relationship with an addict. I was totally alone, and it was happening all over again! I had put all my hopes into this last treatment. I thought he was healed, and our family would be healed. I had stayed because I thought it was what I was supposed to do. I did not set boundaries or hold him accountable or do any of the things an addict needs from his family. I tried desperately to just be enough, make him love us enough to make it all go away. But that does not work with an addict, you can never be enough. The drug is bigger and always will be. Deep down I knew I should have left or made him leave early on.

This moment in the hotel room was when it all hit me like a ton of bricks, even though we had bounced from house to house, and now been in a hotel for six months. I had convinced myself it was temporary, and he was better, and we were on our way out of this mess! As I shut the door after speaking to the hotel manager, it all came to me like a movie playing in my mind. We were homeless, no more denial! Not only were we homeless, but I was totally alone. He was not better; he had left us there and was not coming back to help me. So once again I shoved the tears down as far as I could so my babies did not see how broken I was. I parked the van as close to the back door as I could, and we made a game out of carrying all our things down and loading them into it. When I think of this day, I still cannot believe how I did it. All our possessions in the world were piled in that hotel room, I had three kids under five, one being an infant, and our hotel room was on the third floor. I had no one to call, and no one to help. I guess I could have asked one of the strangers I had met at the hotel. But I could not out of embarrassment. This was my fault because I was not good enough, I was not enough to keep him from doing it and putting us in this position.

WHY DID I FEEL SO WORTHLESS AND NOT GOOD ENOUGH?

My mother was only seventeen when I was born a very tiny premature baby of less than 3lbs. I was not able to leave the hospital until I was almost three months old. Neonatal units were not what they are these days. As a child, I believed she hated me. She treated me as if she could not stand me unless my father or another family member was around. I was the root of all her problems. This got worse as I got older, she put me down every day, called me names I did not even understand. She would lie to my father and make up bad things that I did so he would be upset with me. I never stood up for myself and spoke up, I accepted it and dealt with whatever punishment came. I craved acceptance and attention. This trend followed me in school as well. When I reached the years of high school drama, instead of fighting it, I played along. When rumours would happen, as they inevitably do in high school, I never stood up for myself or denied anything. I would just play along and deal with whatever transpired. At least people were noticing me. To this day, my friends, family and most of all my father do not really know me or what I did and did not do.

After becoming a mother myself, I believed that the separation from my mother contributed to her lack of connection with me as a child. I knew there had to be other problems, as her behaviour just did not make sense. I felt a lot of it was my fault as I was not good enough to behave the way she expected. I did not realise the depth of mental illness she was struggling with until much later.

During the years that followed the end of my marriage, I chose to work primarily in childcare and later as a preschool teacher for several reasons. One, I loved kids and was good at it, and two, it allowed me the flexibility with my schedule I needed as a single mom of six! But this profession would not pay the bills and support my family as I was on my own financially. I worked several jobs for a few years trying to dig out of the financial mess I had been left in. In my early twenties I had been in the health and fitness industry as an aerobics instructor and then personal trainer. So, I went back to that as it was something I loved. I took on personal training clients and taught a bootcamp at my church in the wee hours of the morning (4.30/5am) then I would rush to shower and dress, get the kids ready and off to school, then work at the preschool during the day until school was out. I would go home and spend an hour or so with the kids and get dinner going. Then I would be off to my evening job waiting tables. This was a horrible schedule and I was exhausted all the time, literally wasting away skinny. Yet at the same time, I felt a power for the first time. I had taken control; I was succeeding at providing for my family. I was proud of myself.

A year or two later, I had been able to buy my first home, a new car and had a successful day-care/preschool running out of my home. I knew entrepreneurship was the way to go. Working for someone else was never going to provide enough income for my family. Things were going well; we were surviving through every month, but I was down to my last five dollars after paying the bills. I knew I had reached the max my business would ever produce as an in-home business. I searched and investigated every home-based opportunity I could to give me a second income and possibly savings for my family. I had always been a believer in the power of network marketing and had been a part of a few companies over the years. But I always had an internal struggle of not feeling as good as other people in the company. At the same time, I had a strong feeling I was meant for more.

I joined about seven companies. It would always end the same way. I would dive in headfirst on fire with a deep belief it was going to work. I would find some success and be on my way up the ranks. Then an obstacle would come, and I would allow the voices of other people to sneak back into my head, telling me I was not good enough and I would never achieve the level of success I wanted. I would make up excuses and quit. This cycle was only reaffirming the limiting belief of not being good enough. Fast forward several years and I found myself in yet another network marketing business quite by accident. I started out only looking for some savings for my family and maybe a little extra money on the side. This time, I was not desperate for money. But, of course, after getting started and seeing some of the income that was taking place in the company, I once again got that network marketing bug! I got super excited and motivated to build that business I always knew I was capable of but never achieved. I had a goal of hitting a certain rank within the company and smashed it quickly. But soon after, some of the same patterns began to appear. I was not about to let this happen again. I spent time trying to figure out why I was uneasy, why I was allowing those voices to start sneaking back in; I was not the same needy single mom anymore. So, why was this happening? *Look at the success you just had, you can do this*, I told myself.

I convinced myself that it was just a problem with the process in which I was building my business. I just did not like the spammy ways that everyone was teaching and using online. Even though this is true, and I still feel this way, looking back, I knew in my heart it was a lot deeper than that.

I went on the search for new strategies and programmes to teach me how to do business a new way. Still thinking this was the only problem! I went through several programmes and learned a lot about marketing my business using social media. With every new skill I learned, I thought after I finished each one and applied it to my business, it was going to take off! I was so task orientated. Each time, nothing happened, no movement at all! Within the programme I was in they often posted things about mindset. I usually skipped right over them. I did not have a mindset problem. I knew I was a positive person and absolutely knew I could be successful after I just learned this bot or got my funnel in place! I just knew it, but I was wrong. Something was blocking my success! The thoughts started creeping in again, it is just YOU! You are not good enough.

The group I was in started shifting a bit and there was more and more talk about mindset and challenges to help remove what was blocking you in your business. I finally thought, *Well what the hell*. Still not thinking I had any issues here, I decided to participate anyway. I started doing some of the recommended meditations, etc. and soon realised that I had limiting beliefs that had been holding me back all these years. I could now see clearly how I had been holding myself back simply because I did not believe I was good enough and had zero confidence in my abilities because I had been told all my life I was not good enough. Everything that had happened to me throughout my adult life just kept reinforcing those limiting beliefs.

Now, I have come full circle and I can tell you with no doubt in my mind what my future holds. I know that I can do anything I put my mind to. I create my own reality and no longer allow the ghost of people in my past telling me I am not good enough to control my life. I know that the most important thing in my business is my mindset and it needs to be top priority. #1 in my DMO every day! We are always learning and growing. Entrepreneurship is an amazing journey not only in business and providing an amazing income, time freedom and the financial security everyone dreams about but, most importantly, it is a journey to self-discovery and becoming the person you were put here to be!

I do not tell this story of my past to gain anyone's sympathy. I tell it to reach the one woman that needs to hear it today and inspire her to never give up! We all have a story; we all go through tough times in our lives. Even your mentors or the people you see online that you look up to and think they really have their sh** together! The magic happens when you decide to do the inner work and get to the bottom of what limiting belief is blocking you. We all have them! Do not give up until you find and release yours.

In this last year, my passion has changed from wanting to build a six or seven figure empire to helping as many women as I can to realise their potential and to stop letting their limiting belief of not being good enough make them quit before they even get started. Through this, my empire will come!

★★★

You can find Debbie here:

https://www.facebook.com/debbiepatrickworldwide/
https://www.instagram.com/debbiepatrickworldwide/
https://www.debbiepatrickworldwide.com/

# Listen to the Story of Your Soul
## *Elly Charles*

*I am dedicating my story to the shining light within each and every one of us. The shining light that guides us to our soul's purpose.*

Oh my fucking life, I cannot do this, I'm going to die… are the thoughts running through my mind as I stand at the edge of a plane 15,000 feet in the air strapped to a radical man who has stood here hundreds of times before, with no fear in the world, it's just simple to him!

As I find myself being shuffled closer and closer to the edge of this open door and all I can see are the clouds down below, there is no time to change my mind. For fuck's sake, Elly, why are you doing this in the first place, just get a grip. Then suddenly I'm free falling at the speed of 160 miles per hour. Falling through the sky, I realise why people do this. In that sixty seconds of free falling, all those fears leave me, and I realise that I'm okay. In fact, I'm better than okay, I'm ALIVE, fully and truly alive – and everything is fucking fantastic.

That moment I was fearing so much is the moment I

took the next step to conquering a huge fear of mine. Of course, heights are a big fear of many, but it wasn't really the fear of heights that was holding me back, it was the fear in my mind that I couldn't do it.

Yes, how many have had this fear of *I cannot do it*? Crazy that such thoughts can hold us back.

So, this sixty second free fall was the ultimate moment for me to really realise exactly what I have truly achieved in the last three years, especially the last nine months in particular.

You see, over these last few years, I have achieved so much in my spiritual journey, which then led me to create a wonderful spiritual business called Light After Life that I love so much. Better yet, my transformation has now led me to achieving physical things that I used to find limiting, just like jumping out of a plane. Six months ago, I climbed a temple in the middle of a Mexican jungle and yet again extreme anxiety was holding me back. Halfway through the climb, I looked down and realised I was above the jungle trees and this old temple was just getting higher and higher. I somehow managed to get up to the top and they were right. It was worth it. Yes, because it was so beautiful and peaceful, but also because I had actually achieved it. I HAD DONE IT.

So how did I get from having a drug addiction and absolutely no money with severe depression to now flying freely through the sky achieving and experiencing amazing activities and places as well as helping hundreds of people all over the world? Well, let me tell you a not so little story…

Let's go back to when I was twenty-six and had just moved. I was in the process of getting clean from my cocaine addiction. Living in this tiny little flat in a town I didn't know, I had shut myself off from all the people I knew and, in a way, shut myself away from my own life. I was left to pick up the pieces of the destruction I had caused for so long. No one was interested in helping me anymore because I had burnt my bridges with everyone. My photography business had failed, and I had no money. In fact, I owed lots of money to so many people. The deep heavy feelings so rooted inside of me pulled me back, yet I knew I had to trust in something. That something was the light. This light my mum had always told me about. The light from my angels, the light that sang to my soul and I had to believe, I just had to believe that something was going to change.

As I would lock myself away, realising I had nothing, I began to focus on this pure white light; it got stronger and stronger. I always had strong spiritual senses, so I knew what was happening, but little did I know that this light would be what changed my life forever and was the beginning of a massive transformation into my new life that now flows so freely.

I remember cutting myself when I was in my cloud of depression, cutting myself in between my thighs just so I could get this pain out. I would look in the mirror and be disgusted with myself that I could ever have done what I did over those years of intoxicating my body so badly.

I now know that all of that which held me back in

life was simply pain I felt from my upbringing, mainly from sexual abuse as a child, and this then created a big stench bomb of self-destruct that later in life caused me to have serious blocks in all areas, including my career.

You see, I never felt like I fitted in. No matter what job I had, it just didn't feel right, I always felt unfulfilled. I would feel so sick at the thought of even going into work. I became fed up with working in dead-end jobs, so I had tried to set up a photography business. It did go well at times; however, because of my party life and drug taking, it never worked fully because I was always more interested in getting fucked – WHY? To take the pain of my past away. Of course, I didn't realise that back then.

Eventually, my photography business became non-existent. Don't get me wrong, I was still a brilliant photographer, however it just didn't feel right, it didn't excite me. I began to meditate more and more in my little flat on my own and over the months I found that instead of wanting to cut myself and tell myself horrid things, I started to tell myself that I loved myself. I was focusing on that light I saw and I trusted. I started to become aware of loved ones that had passed over sitting with me and showing themselves to me. They looked so beautiful and glowing. I could hear them, they brought me comfort. They started to show me little snippets of my future. I would ask them to guide me and I would give thanks to them for healing me.

Little by little, I started to venture out of my flat, feeling stronger and stronger. Slowly but surely, things started to change. It took a process of three years from deciding to get clean to realising that I felt like a new woman. Our pain goes deep and we peel the layers back. I found that so many layers were being healed at different stages. It was confronting, but this light was keeping me going.

Now I understand why I had to go through so much hard work and pain. Because I am a light worker and I needed to have these lessons in life to be able to clear this out and understand what it's like to truly heal myself so I can help to heal and guide others.

Fast forward three years from that little flat, I was now twenty-nine years old. I find myself in my new home with my daughter who is nearly two years old. I'm a single mum now, heartbroken over the split with my daughter's father, feeling very lost. I had the choice to either go back to intoxicating myself and going downhill, which at that time was very tempting; when you have had an addiction there is always a part of it that remains with you. Or I could actually listen to this pull to the spiritual realm of what I felt so strongly. So, sure enough, I was strong and listened to that pull. I was already in spiritual development circles and decided to start doing readings for people for a small donation of my time. I would spend three hours in the evening when my daughter was in bed, focusing on practising reading people's energy and connecting to spirit linked to them. Very quickly, people that I was practising on were starting to tell their friends about me and I started to have people I didn't know contacting me for readings. So I decided to start charging a set fee of £15 per person. After a while of doing this, I found myself drawn to set up a business page and I then chose to register my business. I decided to call my business Light After Life because it felt right within my heart. From doing my mediumship, I realised I had a beautiful connection with souls passed over and a great deal of respect for spirit. I saw that their light still shone so brightly even though their physical form had gone and again the light that I trusted in so much felt important to include in my business name. So here when I created the name I was listening to my soul and respecting spirit for I am a messenger to help connection through different light beings earth bound and passed over to continue forward. I felt it was pumping so much positive energy into my business when I chose the name and I still do.

Within the first seven months I had over one hundred five-star reviews on my business page but even then I still didn't realise just what I had achieved. All I knew was that I really enjoyed doing readings for people and the significance I got from spirit blew me away. I began to understand more why I was doing this, and I realised it was because I was helping people and it was helping me and my pain too. One year into offering the readings as a spiritual service, I set up a class. This was something that my grandmother, who is my lovely spirit guide, was giving me visions about and telling me I needed to sort it out. It took me about four months to finally listen to her and actually do it. When I did, I thought it would just be a little circle similar to the ones I had attended a few years back when it began, but seventeen people had booked on. Now to some that may not seem much, but to me I was over the moon. I found myself feeling very overwhelmed that so many turned up. That class turned from one class into eight different classes in different locations and still runs now.

Learning during that next year how to teach and what to teach and also how to understand people from a teacher/student basis was a HUGE turning point for my career and how to be with people. There were times where I felt very energised and excited but there were also times where I felt stressed, for I found that I was going above and beyond to help people and that actually I had no time to just be with my heart. So another big part of my lesson was to make sure that what I am doing is always feeling good for me.

So around this year into teaching and two years into setting up Light After Life, I began to realise OH FUCK people actually want to hear what I have to say, PEOPLE TRUST IN ME. Sounds silly but having that realisation was so profound because I realised that even though I was doing a good job and I felt good about my work, I still had this belief that I was worthless.

When I realised this, it gave me a great boost, not in an egotistical way, but in a really authentic REAL way. This helped me to transform my business even more and let both sides of my business grow. I had started to expand online and was already offering one-to-one sessions for students who did not want to be in a group setting, so I was teaching people effectively all over the world. People were coming from left, right and centre to have readings with me or to be taught by me. Since then I have created my membership The School of Spirituality, which focuses on helping others to trust in their intuition and find their true purpose along their spiritual path as well as focusing on psychism and mediumship. I am very proud of this membership.

You see, what I have realised through meeting and teaching so many amazing people is that everyone has a story to tell. Some of us may get stuck and be stuck for a long time, some of us may never get through it, but some of us find a way to move through it and even forgive the ones that hurt us. The ones that abused us or lied to us.

When you forgive, you set yourself free. That is what I did, I forgave. I realised that through my pain I found my power. Through my readings I gave people the space to just be. Through my teachings I helped others to overcome their pain and to realise that they are not crazy.

Understanding why certain things have happened in your life is the biggest lesson of all. Now through all the feel-good vibes I had whilst creating my business, I had, without realising, raised my vibration to a higher level. So, I was finding more and more positive people coming into my life and more positive opportunities appearing. Doors were opening, I was being recognised for the work I was doing, which was simply just my TRUTH of who I was. My purpose in this lifetime feels amazing. I found that I was even being nominated in things like *The Soul & Spirit Magazine* Awards and I was actually placing in the finalists.

I started to believe maybe there is something in this 'believe and you shall receive' stuff. Not only that, I found that financially I was doing a lot better too. I was able to heal the old money patterns I had from way back during my drug days. It used to haunt me, however now I was in a frequency of believing that my spirit guides would help me get along in life. I'm not greedy, money is just a transfer of energy, but I realised YES I DO DESERVE MONEY. The money I received from my work I would put straight back into my business to progress even further. I happily pay out for other services or bills now because I know money will come back. Everything is a transfer of energy. Absolutely everything.

Another psychic said to me back in February of 2020 that two years ago I would have never imagined achieving all that I have and it took me aback because again it shook me and made me think, *Fuck he's right.* I cry with joy at how far I have come and what I have achieved, especially from that young girl who got so messed up because of the mistakes from adults around her, to the drug-intoxicated young woman that was still so fucked up, trying to heal her inner child, to now a soulful woman loving life. Knowing my roots and where I've come from always helps me to be on top of who I am as a woman.

People have their contracts in life and it's down to us to accept and acknowledge ours. As I said, through our pain, we can find positive power and I saw that in the white light that I decided to trust all those years ago. That light kept me going, it got brighter and brighter and through the darkness I shone. I decided to RISE. I took on my contract.

I feel so lucky that I was guided to create a business that sings to my soul and lifts so many up in a positive way. It's not a job to me, it's my life, my business is ME.

For anyone out there who feels lost, who feels stuck within the trauma of their past, who questions 'Can I ever get through this', or 'Is this really my life', just know that you have your light too and you CAN find it. Your light is waiting to guide you. Switch it on because this is your truth.

Your light is your soul and your soul has work to do.
Find your path, do what you are destined to do.
Believe and you shall RECEIVE.

★★★

You can find Elly here:

Website
https://ellycharlesmediumship.com/
The School of Spirituality
https://ellycharlesmediumship.com/spirituality-2/
Facebook page
https://m.facebook.com/ellycharlesmediumship
Instagram
https://www.instagram.com/lightafterlife?r=nametag

# Always Believe In Your Soul

## Helen Adams

*This chapter is dedicated to Francisca Antonia da Silva Souza, thank you for your consistent support, love and encouragement. May you step forward and realise those dreams that you always had inside you.*
*To Natasha and Jo, for enabling me to see and believe how much I was really capable of, and helping me to take big steps to turn my life around when all seemed lost. I am eternally grateful to you both.*
*And to every empowered woman out there who has that burning desire to blaze her own trail, create her dream business and live life on her own terms, keep following your soul, stay inspired and committed to your mission to having that positive impact on the world.*

Have you ever had a big dream, that when you thought about it, it almost took your breath away? Or a knowing that you are meant to be doing something way bigger than what you are doing right now? That's your soul speaking to you, giving you a glimpse of what is out there… if you have the courage to believe and follow where it takes you.

I had that knowing from a young age. I grew up in a little town where everyone knew everyone else's business, but I always had that deep-down feeling that I wouldn't be staying there forever and I'd move to somewhere more exciting and blaze my own trail. I used to stand in front of the mirror with a hairbrush, singing or talking, and I'd fall asleep at night dreaming of stepping out onto a big stage with hundreds of people cheering and applauding.

When I was thirteen, I wanted to go to stage school in London, but my parents had other ideas. "Acting won't give you a secure income," they said. "You'd be far better off going to uni and getting a good job." I couldn't argue… they were only doing what they thought was best for me, but deep down I hated the fact that I couldn't follow my dream. However, I was determined that that would be the first and the last time that I'd let a burning desire pass me by.

Has anyone ever told you to quit your dream and get a nine to five job? Keep opening your mind and listening to the voice of your soul. It always knows the way!

So, I went to uni, got married, and the happiest moment of my life was when my son was born. But the happiness soon turned to disbelief when I discovered his father was cheating on me. Not long afterwards, I found myself alone with my baby, but I was determined to create a strong future for us both.

I then got the chance to fulfil my second passion and twelve months later I qualified as a teacher. It was so rewarding to see my students having lightbulb moments and the proudest day of my career was when the little primary school orchestra I started from scratch won a silver medal in its first competition. At the end of that term, though, I knew it was time for a change. I was ready to make a bigger impact... but how?

One important lesson that we learn on our soul journey is to let go of the how and just trust, then the signs will be presented to us. I was sitting in my lounge a few days later, when I looked over at my bookcase and was drawn to a book called *Be Your Own Life Coach*. I took the book off the shelf and as I held it in my hands I felt a warm, glowing feeling in my body. This was definitely the sign I had been waiting for! Coaching ticked all the boxes. I could help people move forward and make great shifts in their lives and businesses, with far more scope, but better still, coaching could give me the chance to speak on those big stages that I'd dreamed of as a kid. At the back of the book were details on how to qualify as a coach. I checked out the website and signed up for the course.

When we receive these lightbulb moments, we need to act on them without delay, however scary that may be. Natasha of the Femalepreneurs Academy has a favourite saying, "You go first and the Universe follows!" These big dreams are all out there waiting for us, but we have to make the first move and take those steps to make them happen. It's all too easy to destroy them in minutes by second guessing yourself and allowing the doubt to set in.

I soon realised that I needed to spread my wings, so

I left the little town with my son to start a new life in a big city. Not everyone agreed with my decision, but I was determined. I quickly began to understand that making determined decisions is a vital part of success… not everyone will like what you do, and often those people are the ones who are closest to you. But first and foremost, you have to be true to yourself and follow your soul.

I'd been in education for many years, but I'd definitely say that my biggest teacher in life was running my own business. It made me grow and level up in a way that school never could. My business journey took me on all kinds of experiences – having clients, going for weeks without any interest, coming into contact with people who genuinely wanted to help me and others who wanted nothing more than to make a quick buck out of me. The first few clients came to an end, and because I had no knowledge of strategy or marketing, I started to panic. I needed more income. Where was it going to come from? Every time I thought of going back to nine to five, something inside me rejected it. I was hooked on the idea of being my own boss, even though I had a long way to go.

The answer was presented to me a few weeks later at a networking meeting. Over breakfast, one of the other members of the group, a style coach, told me about her second business. This was my very first introduction to network marketing. I found it incredible that regardless of a person's background, they could make the amount of money that they chose, not be dictated to by a boss, or "know the right people" to achieve the goals and dreams they really desired. I decided to use some of my money to buy a ticket to the next Success Day, attended by people from all over the country. I was captured by the vibrant atmosphere, moved by some of the stories from the speakers, and pleasantly surprised to see regular five-figure per month earners laughing, chatting and offering advice to total beginners. Of course, I knew that this wasn't a "get rich quick scheme", but it gave me an idea of what was possible. I knew I'd have to work hard to achieve my dreams, and this could definitely be a way of getting me there.

After a few months, though, I was to learn another lesson – the importance of protecting your energy and your vision. I wasn't moving forward with this new business. In fact, I'd only had a handful of orders since I'd started. People had begun mentioning to me that I was involved in a "pyramid scheme", that those at the top made all the money, and that very few beginners succeeded. In fact, some of these well-meaning folk went so far as to say that they were deluding people! Being new to the industry, my confidence started to dwindle away, and I remembered my mother's words, "Never invest in a business as you'll lose all your money, the only security is in a nine to five job." Does that sound familiar?

Three network marketing companies later, I was sure I'd found "the one". I was absolutely in love with the products, and this time I had managed to build up a small but productive team. When I thought about it, those other two companies hadn't been failures but learning experiences. They'd enabled me to discover what I didn't want, they kept me going in search of what I did want and built up my resilience. And I was rewarded. I can still remember that breath-taking night where I smashed my next rank with literally five minutes to spare, which meant I would get to go on stage at the next national event. Maybe my strategy hadn't improved that much, but my determination was certainly making up for it!

Two weeks later, as I stood on the stage, I felt that glow of pride and excitement, and I knew I wanted more of it. I saw my team applauding me and it reminded me of all those dreams I had growing up all those years ago. It was such a special day for me, and I loved being able to celebrate with my team who had worked so hard. I couldn't wait to be back there the following year with my next promotion.

Once again, though, the school of business was to teach me some hard but valuable lessons. Nobody will ever care for your business the same way you do. It's pointless trying to get them to do so. The next month, two of my team decided to leave. After all the momentum from the month before, the ones who were left were unable to repeat that performance. I lost my status the following month, and to say that I was gutted was an understatement.

How could everything go so wrong in a matter of weeks? I decided to break everything down. These are the things I realised:

1. To be a good leader, your job is to SERVE your team. To really understand their wants, needs and personalities. And to get them to use their strengths through the business to make these wants and needs a reality.
2. In the first instance, each member of your team will be working for THEMSELVES, not for the team. "Smashing a target for the team" is very rarely a motivator.
3. Consistency is key. Don't stop doing what got you there in the first place.

I didn't want to listen to these messages coming from my intuition. I was too busy feeling sorry for myself. My vibe dropped lower, my ex decided to leave me, and I wrote off my beautiful Audi that I'd only bought a year before. By this time, my son had left home. I was alone. And I needed money. After the euphoria of the month before, I now felt like a total and utter failure. But I couldn't sit there and feel sorry for myself. I had to get on with my life.

My next year was spent working as a care assistant. It was so rewarding to see the smiles on the clients' faces. I used to love laughing and joking with them. But I knew deep down that this wasn't where I was meant to be. The dreams kept coming back. It was my soul reminding me that I should be taking the steps to do what I really wanted to do.

There's an old saying, "When the student is ready, the teacher will appear." I remembered in my early days of coaching, some of my coach friends used to talk about the Universe and the Law of Attraction. I was feeling drawn to learn more about it, so I re-read *The Secret* and other books, and started to watch YouTube videos. I began to make meditation part of my morning routine and could not believe how clear I felt at the end of each session. My intuition was opening right up and for the first time in a long time I started to feel aligned. And then one day when I was meditating, I became aware of my soul's purpose. I was to empower women worldwide, and coach them to live a life on their own terms. I closed my eyes and saw myself sitting at a table with some women, sharing my knowledge with them, and then the scene changed to me stepping out onto a stage to deafening applause. At last, that dream was making sense. Public speaking was to be a big part of my mission and would help me reach those millions of women all around the globe. I felt that warm glow inside me once again. I was definitely in tune with my soul!

Once you're on your soul journey, there's no turning back. However, one thing I hadn't prepared myself for was the inner work. When you're enjoying that amazing feeling of being on a high and then out of nowhere a massive fear rises up inside you, it knocks you for six. Or, all of a sudden, the imposter syndrome kicks in. This isn't a signal to give up, it's a signal to show you that your limiting beliefs are coming up to the surface to be released. As you grow more and more, you will dig deeper and deeper and peel more and more layers off until you get to the truest version of you in all your glory!

I started a new Facebook group and invited a few women, doing lives and offering free trainings to make it grow. I even created a one-day course, which I was quite proud of. The first time I ran it, two ladies came to my home and took part, and got breakthroughs. One even enrolled on a course that she'd been wanting to do for over thirty years!

Over the next few months, though, things started to turn sour again. Even though the group was growing, I was struggling to get people on the paid courses. The money started trickling out of my bank account, my new office became a table at Wetherspoons with refillable coffee, and sometimes when I needed to message people I'd drive to a nearby pub car park and sit there on my phone. The easy option would have been to go back to nine to five but something inside was stopping me once again. I'd been given my mission. Now I had to make it work.

For a couple of years, I'd been following Natasha and Jo and had absolutely fallen in love with their brand of strategy and soul. My intuition told me to reach out to Jo as she would be able to help me. We worked together on creating my new brand, getting crystal clear on my audience and developing a high-ticket programme. I dove into the tasks she set me with enthusiasm and cried tears of joy when my first client signed up to my £500 programme. At last I had a strong, effective strategy that I could use over and over again and make that impact I truly came here to make.

As I look back on my journey, the biggest thing

I learned is to follow your soul without hesitation, as it'll always keep nudging you until you do. And make those bold decisions with strength and courage because each one of them will take you a step nearer to that strong, empowered female leader you always dreamed of becoming.

★★★

You can find Helen here:

https://linktr.ee/helenlouiseadams

# Why Me?
## Katie Yarham

*I have a massive amount of appreciation for my mum and dad for always being there for me, despite not being together. Dad, thank you for teaching me that 'normal' doesn't exist and for showing me love by not telling me what I wanted to hear. Saying no to the Magnum ice cream on the occasional Sunday has stood me in good stead too! And Mum, you've guided me to become the woman I am today, and I can't thank you enough for the years of love you've shown me, even when you've found things tough yourself. Scott, you are one amazing man for staying by my side over the past twenty years. It mustn't have been easy to see me fall apart mentally and physically but you've never taken a second thought about putting me first and supporting me through my challenging times. I can't wait to make the next twenty years the best yet! I love you so much. And to my girls, you know who you are. Long nights listening to my woes, consoling me during dark times and never giving up on me. I love you all*

If I shut my eyes, I can remember and feel the pain, every knot in my stomach, my mouth as dry as an old leather belt and the sick feeling that just wouldn't go away. The freezing cold dark journey home in the snow from the office took me down a road where I thought there was no way of escaping the hurt, turmoil and disbelief that had developed again. This third episode of anxiety and depression was enough. I couldn't take any more. I wanted to end it. That tree ahead, the one I always drove past on the way home from work looked like the best solution to heal my sadness. Wrap my car around it and bam! No more chances to get kicked in the teeth, be manipulated and treated like a piece of shit again.

'Why me?' continually ran through my head. I'm a friendly, giving, honest, reliable and empathetic soul who loves to be loved. Was that the problem causing my mental health issues? Was I expecting too much from people? Did I not deserve to be happy? I must have done something wrong in my past. Was it normal for me to be burdened with anxiety and depression, seeing as my dad had struggled with mental health all through his adult working life, to the point where he had to take early retirement? You see, blame is the easy way out. When your head is messed up, logic legs it! So much so, the suicidal thoughts crept in and this was confirmed during mental health appointments for cognitive behavioural therapy. Bloody hell, this was real, I was losing it.

Actually no! How could I be causing all this pain? Bullying was what happened to Katie, with the first experiences of name-calling, being ignored and left out and feeling absolutely worthless, starting in middle school. All because I had protruding teeth. My mum and dad when they were together made the decision not to give me a dummy when I was a baby, so my thumb was my comforter. But unfortunately, I didn't grow out of this habit and it caused my teeth to stick out. So, what do you do? You get top and bottom braces, after having about six teeth pulled out. And guess what? I was bullied for having 'train tracks' in my face!

But it didn't stop there. If there was a 'teacher's pet' or 'square head' at school then according to the bullies who made my life hell, I was her. Thinking back to the middle school years, I remember often being picked last for team sports like rounders, although I was one of the fastest runners, even amongst the boys. On another occasion, during a school trip to Bognor Regis, my so-called friends decided not to hang around with me, so I was a Billy no mates. One girl used to swing her bum-length ponytail around her head and whack me with it. The pain was like a wasp sting, but it wasn't that which really hurt, it was the embarrassment in front of the other kids.

I was completely torn to bits in my mind. I loved to learn and usually looked forward to going to school and I know that my mum, dad and family were utterly proud of me, the achievements I made and the girl I was growing up to be. I enjoyed the attention and reassurance I received when I was doing well but, at the same time, I got a massive buzz from helping my friends feel the best that they could. It just didn't make sense. How could helping others be such a bad thing in some of the other children's eyes?

But this memory still to this day completely saddens

me. My Grandad Barrie (Gramps) taught me to play the clarinet in his garden shed when I was about seven. Music was, and still is my Gramps' life and it had begun to be a big part of mine, alongside my dancing lessons in ballet, tap and modern. I went out of my comfort zone many a time, for exams and shows, for both hobbies. Before long I was the tiny girl with long socks, nestled in the middle of the older clarinet players that had taken me under their wing in the school orchestra. I was a little fish in a big pond. But I won't forget the day that broke my heart.

I was meant to be playing in the High School orchestra, on stage, in front of the whole school. I was petrified that I'd get bullied again for being a 'square', so I deliberately forgot to take my Gramps' clarinet to school with me that morning so that I could get out of it. I never picked up the clarinet again. Gramps, if you are reading this, I want you to know how much I loved our time together and I will always cherish these good memories.

Fast forward through my years at college completing A Levels, to my time at university studying for a Psychology (Hons) degree, I really did start to flourish. I didn't feel like I had to fit in, and I developed what turned out to be some healthy and long-lasting friendships. I even reconnected with an old first school friend who was doing the same degree as me. That was an amazing surprise! Suddenly, I felt like things were falling into place.

I'd also been in a relationship with Scott (my now

husband of ten years, partner for twenty years) for about three years and things were going really well. Until Scott, out of the blue, ended it! Right when I was working through my 10,000-word dissertation to enable me to finish my degree! I was devastated and can even remember to this day the sadness I felt and the Delta Goodrum CD album that I played over and over again to try and cry out my pain. My poor mum didn't know what to do with me and, for the life of me, I didn't know why this was happening again. This was the third time I'd been dumped, right when I was finishing my studies. First doing my GCSEs, then my A Levels and now this.

But somehow, I found the strength to put my all into my studies and asked for help, where my tutor granted me mitigating circumstances and an extension. By the skin of my teeth I submitted my dissertation. After the panic and desperation of the whole ordeal, I sat on the bus to come home, shaking. I felt sick and disconnected from my body. Writing this now, and only just now, has made me realise that this may well have been my first experience of anxiety and I didn't even know it at the time.

The thought of a rewarding career was what I wanted. I spoke with Scott a lot about me not wanting to have children (I never had done growing up) and he was 100% happy with this. My career was going to be my baby. Well, so I thought. I knew since middle school that I wanted to work in some kind of teaching/support role. So, after graduating, I was so excited to start my first 'proper' job as a Learning Support Assistant. I was absolutely buzzing and ready to take on the world. Yet little did I know at the time that I was to be faced with challenges that previous one-to-one assistants experienced. To the extent where many employees felt the need to resign because they couldn't cope. Nevertheless, I gave it a go.

What is so sad, looking back, is that I was being manipulated again but by the child I was actually meant to be supporting. My experiences of childhood bullying were repeating themselves again. But the student couldn't help it. I was the one who was meant to have my shit together and help. I felt ashamed for feeling out of my depth, feeling scared of the child and even out of control. I felt useless and a let-down.

I remember hiding away in the toilet at the Pupil Referral Unit, sobbing quietly on the loo with my hands smothering my mouth so that nobody else could hear, with sweaty hands, feeling hot yet cold at the same time. My trousers and top would stick to me with the cold sweatiness. That knot in my stomach and the lump in my chest and throat were everyday occurrences. Unlike being able to ask my uni tutor for help, I just couldn't bring myself to tell my colleagues how I felt. In fact, they were all so incredibly talented, dedicated and passionate. Because I had studied modules in Child Psychology and Abnormal Psychology at uni, I was meant to be the 'expert'. The staff didn't think this, I did. I always felt that I had to be good at everything I tried. Failure wasn't an option to me.

These feelings of stress and anxiety went on for months until I crumbled. I was completely gobsmacked when the doctor diagnosed me with anxiety and stress, signing me off work for six weeks. Mentally and physically I was exhausted and needed to regroup. I had no idea what to do to overcome this pain. A change of path was what I needed. So, here I was having left the school on a good note, briefly trying a post-graduate course in Human Resources (I binned that off!) and having worked in a handful of admin roles (something that wasn't on my agenda when I graduated), afraid of answering the telephone in case I faced confrontation. I had zero confidence. I always felt nervous of doing things wrong and people shouting at me.

In all the admin jobs I've had, I've always declared experiencing anxiety/depression. At the end of the day, employers should have policies in place that are implemented and followed to support employees with mental health conditions, as much as the next employee who has a bad back, right? NO! This doesn't happen in the real world. I can't go into details (and now isn't the place) but let's just say that the human element in Human Resources was bullshit! The tangled webs of lies, back-stabbing and cover ups were plain to see. I just didn't have the strength to follow through with the Employment Tribunal. I had to let it go, I had to lose my voice, I had to lose the opportunity for sharing my story. I knew I had a strong case with the hard evidence that I had, but my mind and body was weak.

Thankfully, I had a saviour. Whilst working full-time at the second admin job where I had two breakdowns, I decided to start a Beauty Therapy NVQ Level 2 course, in the evenings, over two years. But that mini intro course I took before taking the plunge really showed me that I was a bag of nerves. It literally felt like those English lessons in school where the teacher goes around the class, making you speak in turn. Where you dread speaking and are embarrassed of the sound of your own voice. I needed to know that this decision was the right one this time. I couldn't take any more shit. I had to get it right.

My little beauty business went from strength to strength over six years and I was now working from home full time! But something was missing. I was in my comfort zone, but I felt strong enough to try something else and I was missing working with others. That skincare brochure my mum-in-law gave me to look at was what kick-started the next chapter.

During the past five years, I've become a new woman, the one I could have been years and years ago. All thanks to me being brave and enquiring about a social selling opportunity. I'm doing things now that I never dreamt of doing. Going to strangers' homes to demonstrate and talk about my love of natural skincare, delivering training and speeches in front of 20–300+ women to share my story to help inspire them. Achieving trips abroad to Lapland, Mauritius, South Africa, Paris, the French Riviera and Barcelona, attending events in a room with 3,000 women and walking on stage to collect rewards for different personal achievements. I can't believe how much my self-belief, confidence and mental health has improved in this time frame. What makes it even more special is that I can help support and inspire other women to start their own beauty businesses through social selling and as a beauty therapist (as I also teach on a freelance basis in this area too), and break free from all the crap they may have encountered. Yet, with three plus whirlwind years of recognition and success came the downward spiral, something that I didn't think could even be possible. Until last year, when I needed to get my shit together yet again.

As can happen in network marketing and life in general, you sometimes have friendships and conversations that were once the most important things to you, and hanging onto every word or experience as though that's the real truth and the best thing for you. I do, especially as I easily trust. But you grow as a person, find your voice, become braver speaking up and going against the norm. I knew I could run my business in a non-traditional way using social media but not everyone agrees.

Last year I fell into a period of depression. My social selling business had taken a dip due to several factors, which happen to the best of us. But I felt like a failure, taking me back to those times working at the school. Obviously, it was an experience that I hadn't fully got over. This time, instead of turning to chocolate for an endorphin boost, it was alcohol and poor self-care. Even Scott didn't know that I'd open a bottle of wine after he went to bed and finish the lot. This happened most nights. I just couldn't face going to bed and many nights I only had about four to five hours sleep. I was scared of having nightmares and waking up feeling worthless. I even cut back doing beauty treatments thinking that was the right thing to do to be successful, yet it felt like my right arm had been cut off. The one thing that made me the happy person that I was and got me out of the office. But I couldn't face putting on a brave face and pretending I was okay, so I'd cancel appointments, arrangements with friends and often lie about the reasons. I thought that nobody would stick by me if I told them the real reason I felt ill. Why would they? When I did tell them in those office jobs, everything was done to try to get rid of me.

So, there you have it, the repetition of situations that keep rearing their ugly heads as you go through your life journey. It hasn't always been domestic or physical abuse that some women sadly go through, the results of which can be visibly seen, but it's been the invisible, to others and often myself. The main things I've learnt over the past year or so, thanks to the support from Natasha Edwards and Jo Jo Ellen, is that the shit times and 'failures' happen for a reason. They are to test us, to ask us if we're happy, to question us if we are in tune with our feelings, if we are on the right life path. And that all the things that our mind absorbs, through the hurtful words, experiences, relationships, jobs, etc., are a reflection of that other person's mind. But it does influence our thoughts, beliefs and emotions.

Now that I've reconnected with my interest in psychology and self-development, using my own belief systems, I'm slowly unearthing the real Katie. The one that Scott wants to cuddle, hold, go on holiday with and see happy. And the Katie that can hold her head high, and be proud of the kind natured, honest, empathetic soul that she is. And doesn't want other women to experience words like, and I paraphrase, "I do think you're using your mental health as an excuse for things."

'Why me?' is a huge, deep and unanswerable question. But what matters the most is that you know deep down that your gut feelings are very rarely wrong. Follow your heart and soul and the rest will follow with you.

★★★

You can find Katie here:

https://www.facebook.com/EABT-at-Karing-Touch-Beauty-Holistic-Training-268670676877743/
https://www.facebook.com/katie.yarham

# For the Silent Voices
## Katy Curry

*I dedicate this chapter to my famalam, you wonderful bunch of humans, thank you for teaching me compassion, kindness and always accepting my free spirit, even when it's made no sense to you. Love you all. Rod, thanks for joining me on this crazy ride we call life, I love you.*
*My message to you all, you are safe, you are loved, you didn't do anything wrong. Let it go, start working on yourself, start putting yourself first and find your peace.*

"Just sit back, relax and let the world pass by."
– Wynn Curry.

I'm writing this chapter to raise awareness of an incredible charity, NOCOA (The National Association for Children of Alcoholics) and the fantastic work they do. There are an estimated 1.7million children in the UK living with an alcohol-dependent parent and 2.8 million adult children who were brought up in a family where one or more parents drank too much. My hope for this chapter is that if you are one of those adults you will allow yourself to see how loved, cared for and safe you are, you can let it go now and you can contact NOCOA if you are struggling with a parent who drinks too much.

Growing up a COA (child of an alcoholic), I often felt lonely and like no one understood me. Knowing everything that I do now about the mind and how we process the world, I'm not surprised. We have thoughts all day, many of them totally automatic and learnt in the first years of our life and programmed in, some are positive and many are negative.

I can't lie, writing 'my story' makes me feel, well, a bit daft. I kind of laugh and think, *Who the fuck am I to be writing my story for a book? Little Katy Curry from Ashington, how did I even end up here?*

I grew up in the North East of England and loved growing up there; it taught me a lot about life and Geordies are some of the nicest and kindest people you ever could meet. Loud, love a drink and have less filters than the rest of the UK, but fun! Drinking, the boozer and going out partying is the culture in the North East, as are men wearing no coat even when it's snowing outside. I never did quite understand that one...

I don't think in my wildest dreams as a lost sixteen-year-old girl I would have thought I'd end up on the career path I have. Mind, I had absolutely no idea what I wanted to do other than at some point move away from my small town and travel the world. I left school at sixteen and went to college to study beauty therapy. I decided then I wanted to be self-employed some day. I got my best buddy Bruce the Jack Russel and decided time was what I wanted. It's taken me almost a decade to find my thing that can get me time freedom but I got there in the end.

My dad has always been my biggest supporter in my entrepreneurial journey and my mum always encouraged following my heart, and for that I'm truly thankful. My first business doing Avon unleashed the inner entrepreneur within me. I realised there were a lot of ways people earned money without needing a job and I wanted me some of that. I don't think my wildflower personality could have ever let me settle for a normal career path in the nine to five and gosh am I glad she didn't.

My journey from that point has led me down many twists and turns from working in the financial services industry for the past eight years alongside studying special effects makeup at university, gaining a childhood and youth studies degree to now becoming an online coach and building a residual income in the travel industry online whilst helping others to do the same. If you aren't creating financial security for yourself now by building multiple income streams, you really should be! I want to open the minds of others to this new way of working online and the incredible opportunities that are out there.

I have to say, gaining a first class degree in childhood and youth studies is still my biggest and my proudest achievement ever. A first class fucking degree, me! It's still totally wild to me! I swear, I definitely manifested that. I certainly didn't realise the healing path doing that degree would set me on or the career path I'd end up with when I started. I had plans to go onto teaching or youth work, I hadn't even heard of coaching at that time.

It wasn't until I wrote a dissertation named "The impact of parental drinking on the adult child of the alcoholic" (it's got an arsey name because I had to twist it around a little to get away with it being on adults and not children) that I realised what a huge problem the UK has with alcoholism and just how many children are suffering in silence whilst dealing with their parents' drinking. Alcoholism in the UK is treated like a dirty secret that no one talks about. Growing up, I truly felt like I was the only one who had a parent who drank too much. No one spoke about it and it wasn't until then that I realised, I really, really, really wasn't the only child who grew up with an alcoholic parent. The subject of alcoholism went from my head to my heart and I knew that, somehow, I was going to have to use this information to help others.

In my study, I asked adult children of alcoholics (ACOAs) what impact they felt their parents' drinking had on them. I had so many responses, some heartbreaking, some sad, others saying their parents' drinking caused them to feel anxious, people please or to feel depressed. Although it did also find that COAs who grow up with a stable parent in their household or in regular contact often are less impacted by their parents' drinking problem – shout out to my mum, grandma Wynn and grandad for being that in my life. Three of the most consistent people in my life growing up.

Although my dad drank A LOT during my formative

years, or nought to seven, I was so lucky to have my mum in my life who did her best to hide it and make life as normal as possible. Honestly, I don't know how she did it and that my dad actually stopped drinking for a large portion of my life. It wasn't until my early twenties that I really experienced life with an alcoholic parent.

I didn't really struggle so badly with my dad, however. I know there are many children out there living in much worse circumstances and there are many adult children who grew up in much worse circumstances and that's why I want to raise awareness on the subject to help and allow those souls to know they're not alone. We hold onto so much of our childhoods, the resentment, pain, the patterns we grew up around, and it's important we know this can be changed, you don't have to carry on the way you are if you just learn to manage your mind and heal your past.

I was really fascinated by the study. I couldn't get my head around this being such a big problem yet it not being spoken about! For some reason, despite alcohol being the main thing in pretty much every household, event or lifestyle, this society that we live in throws alcoholics to the wayside, NEVER to be spoken about. How can something that is legal, highly addictive and pretty much expected in our society then become the word, person and subject that is covered up, brushed under the carpet and barely spoken about once it becomes an addiction in someone's life? It's literally designed to be addictive for the human body.

I don't think a single alcoholic on earth tried their

first cider and decided that they would become an alcoholic, because that's the life they wanted to live and hey, don't alcoholics live the easy life? Just drink all day and do nothing…

Thankfully, I was brought up in a family where it was spoken about and I was reminded by family that it wasn't my fault. My understanding of alcoholism and addiction has grown greatly in the past few years, I have such a deep understanding and compassion for those who struggle with it, but mostly those families and children who also have to deal with it, with very little support and a lot of opinions from the outside. I believe if we had more conversation around this subject and were more open when alcohol moves to alcoholism, many people would struggle less, children would feel safer and heard and we as a society would have more compassion for those affected by it.

Last year, my dad was pretty poorly (he's on the mend now, thankfully) and I'm so grateful that I had already started my personal development and coaching journey and had a toolbox filled to deal with these negative thoughts. I knew I was just experiencing the world from the lessons, values and beliefs I've created over the years and could choose differently. We all have that option in life, but often we can be so hard and negative on ourselves. If you wouldn't say it to your best friend, then you shouldn't say it to you!

I know for a fact coaching and the personal development I had learned saved me whilst my dad was poorly. I'm a soft soul, I always have been. I feel things intensely deeply for myself and for others. I really have no idea how I would've gotten through all of that without them, especially whilst trying to adult, keep my house clean and build an online business.

After finishing my degree and starting back in my nine to five job, I decided I wanted to build an online business. I wasn't sure what, but I just followed my intuition. I'd been learning about manifestation a lot in the previous few years and followed someone online who was a Law of Attraction coach and fell in love with the idea of a career where I could help people and start creating more freedom in my life! I don't think I realised what a personal development journey it was going to be. The online world is incredible and filled with opportunities, but overcoming those fears you have about it can be one big hurdle. Excited and ready to go, I started my online business as a coach, only to realise this wasn't going to be quite as easy as I expected! Roll on the personal development.

As my journey continued, I started learning more about the mind and how our thoughts create our feelings and our feelings create our actions. My grandma had always been super positive in my life and I never really understood how she didn't worry like the rest of us. I've had an anxious mind for as long as I can remember. I realised I'd had a victim mindset for more of my life than I'd like to admit, 'why does this always happen to me', 'life's so unfair', 'why can't I be that pretty', 'nobody likes me', 'I can't do it', 'I'm not clever enough', 'I'll fail before I even start'. Time to change that!

It was a truly empowering moment when I realised it wasn't happening to me, it was happening because of me! My thoughts were creating all of these situations.

I was honestly fascinated; how is this information not taught in schools? I realised how many negative thought patterns I had in my life, I was pretty mean to myself and often thought everything was my fault if something went wrong. Our minds are so fascinating to me and we truly do create our reality through the thoughts, beliefs and actions we take.

We experience most of our reality from the programming we received between the ages of nought and seven. Wild, right? We're basically just all running around being run by our inner child. Our subconscious mind runs this programme and thankfully we can re-programme it!

I began to work on myself tirelessly, reading personal development books, being coached so I could see the world from a different perspective and release negative emotions alongside doing a lot of spiritual healing and inner child work. My trust in myself and my intuition has grown massively and thankfully I can now take action on the things I want in life without all of the drama – well, some of the time, I'm still a work in progress.

As I went deeper with my journey, I deepened my spirituality too. I found some mentors who were into the same kind of vibe as me and started my healing journey. Up until this point, I had lived with a pretty overactive mind, I suffered with social anxiety in my early twenties and I would often worry if I'd said or done the wrong thing.

I've released a lot, healed a lot and what I've come to realise since starting on my healing journey is that not everything is my fault, I don't have to look after and care for everyone, it's okay to fail and try again. The meaning my brain gives my dad's drinking is just the way I perceived it at that moment. It's not his fault, nor mine. My dad was simply doing the best he could, in a time that I'm sure was very hard for him too. I've been able to overcome all these things that held me back for so long, and you can too. I've finally found my voice and I'm ready to be heard.

I feel a deep sense of peace and calm in my life, I'm happy and at peace and peace is all I've ever wanted. My entrepreneurial journey has been a weird and wonderful one and has been more of a personal development journey than anything, but I'm glad I've finally found my thing, didn't give up and now I get to help others to heal and transform their mindset so they can create financial security by building an online income. Trust me, if I can do this, you absolutely can too. I genuinely thought my life was over when I was sixteen and got a D in my English GCSE and here I am writing a chapter for a book. We can create any experience we want if we're willing to work for it.

And that's how I ended up here, writing my story. Yet, somehow, I don't feel like it's just one story, it's all of our story, for you, the silent voices.

It's time to be heard, alcoholism and having a parent,

brother, sister, son, daughter, mother, father, parent, friend, whomever they may be to you, having problems with alcohol is nothing to be ashamed about.

In a society where alcohol is expected to be drunk, can we please create a safe space for those struggling with it and the families impacted to receive help and be supported.

Peace out, KC.

"We're all just out here trying to do our best with the tools we have available to us," – and I think it's important we all remember that a little more.

★★★

You can find Katy here:

www.katycurry.com
www.nacoa.org.uk

# Things Can Always Get Better

## Leanne Willis

*I would like to dedicate this chapter to my mum and dad and sister, for never giving up on me and always being there, no matter what. You're all amazing.*
*To Faith and Max for being my biggest why and my motivation to keep going.*
*To Chris, who has been my biggest supporter and my absolute rock, thank you for showing me and the kids what it's like to have that perfect family.*

Have you ever been at a point in your life when someone looking in from the outside would think, "You have a great life"? I was married with two beautiful children and a successful hair and beauty business. In reality, I was broken, unhappy and tired of being controlled. I couldn't see a way out. I have been so incredibly fortunate to grow up in the most amazingly supportive and loving family; my mum and dad were childhood sweethearts and are still together to this day. This image of the perfect family represented the vision I wanted to create for my family and the security I wanted for my children. Unfortunately for me, this was not the case. I was stuck in a controlling marriage where I was consistently made to feel like I was not good enough, being told what I could and could not do. I knew that I deserved so much more, but he had been chipping away at my confidence for years, so I stayed. Then along came my blessing in disguise. The ultimate betrayal. He cheated and my world had been thrown into chaos.

My dream of a happy family felt further away than ever. I was a shell of my former self; a broken and worn out single mum. I had to raise my daughter Faith who was five and my little boy Max who was nine months old, whilst running a hectic salon and maintaining the home. The stress started to pile on and I didn't handle it in the best way. I was free for the first time in years and I had no one to answer to. I was my own boss and I had my own life.

I had been controlled for so long that I completely rebelled. I was going out partying, drinking and acting like I didn't have a care in the world. What was once fun quickly turned into a lifestyle I couldn't sustain. I was on the verge of losing so much but I didn't know how to stop. I was losing control of myself and everything around me. I had hit the 'self-destruct' button.

I was losing control of my life and this time I had no one else to blame but me. I had lost myself, my self-respect and my self-worth in one swoop. That once confident, focused, driven person was slowly fading away. The way I was living my life and dealing with – or not dealing with – my problems, caused me to hit rock bottom. I was on the verge of giving up on life and I just couldn't see a way out. I was so stressed out that I chose to relieve my stress in a bottle of wine. And then another. I would wake up each morning and think, *Right, today is the day I sort my life out*, but even my daily life became stressful. I was trying to be the best mum I could be, run the salon, and look after the house. It was all too much and instead of finding a way to work through my problems, I shut myself away from the world and drowned my problems. I quickly realised this was not a solution and I was ready to give up on my dream career that I had worked so hard to build. My lifestyle wasn't sustainable, the salon was costing too much money and I felt so low. I didn't think I had it in me to get back up and fight for what I had worked so hard to achieve. I was burnt out. I was tired of trying and failing.

It got to the point where I was feeling so low, yet the bills kept coming. I knew something had to change. This was not the life I wanted, this was not me. I didn't recognise myself. After many thoughtful chats with my mum, dad and boyfriend Chris, I decided to close the salon. I knew it wasn't going to be easy and I was scared of what people would think. Would they think I was a failure? Maybe they did, but I needed to let go before my life went with it.

That was it. Decision made. I attempted to regain control and almost overnight something amazing happened. I felt like a weight had been lifted. Why had it taken me so long to do this? What had I been holding on to? Sometimes we hold on to things so tightly that we cannot see that it is that same thing that we need to let go of.

Life really started to get better from that day. I felt like me for the first time in a long time, and I was starting to get my life back. I knew this wasn't going to be an instant transformation because I still had a lot to deal with. I had thoughts racing through my head and an extreme lack of confidence. For anyone that knows me, they would say low confidence is not something I suffer with; I had hiding my real feelings down to an art. Even though I had a long way to go, I had taken the first step and it felt good.

As this new me started to emerge, many great things started to happen. Things were going really well with Chris and I. He was my rock through so many of my tough moments and I was so grateful to have him in my life. Then one absolutely amazing thing happened: my passion for life was reignited. I was eager to create a better life for my family and that's when I started to feel the need for more. Beauty has always been my dream job. Being self-employed has some amazing advantages and my decision to work at home enabled me to be more present in the kids' lives. Being self-employed also has many disadvantages, such as the long hours and lack of holiday pay (incredibly important in our long-distance relationship).

I started to think about other options. What else could I do to help create more time and more money? That's when I came across network marketing. I remembered my friend Niki, who had messaged me a few months earlier about this new venture that she had started. I read her message asking me to join and I replied, "Yes," putting my phone down and forgetting all about it. In the following days, I was weighing up my options and she suddenly popped into my head. We had a great catch up and she introduced me to this amazing brand that presented so many opportunities – I was blown away. It ticked all the boxes. I wanted the ability to create more time and money whilst working on personal development. She was so full of positivity and excitement about what she was sharing, I got excited too.

Have you ever had that feeling in your tummy when something just feels so right that you can't get it out of your head? That was me. Something was telling me that this was exactly what I needed. I wanted to create my own choices in life, but I also knew I had a lot of growing to do. This seemed the perfect way to do it and wow, I am glad that I did. My network marketing journey had started.

Looking back over the years, I realised that I had already gained experience within network marketing through a number of different opportunities, but none had provided the level of coaching, training and community that I found here. They helped me to see all the opportunities I had been missing out on. How had I missed out on so much? I say it's fate. I am a true believer in everything happening for a reason.

Here I was, getting started on this incredible journey and I loved it. I fell in love with it (and myself). Within a matter of weeks, I had already seen so many changes in myself. The wine-drinking-soap-binging-girl had disappeared, and the TV remained off, as I focused on the vision I wanted to create. Instead of surrounding myself with negativity and self-doubt, I was suddenly surrounded by a community of supportive and uplifting people. People who wanted to see one another succeed and reach their goals. It was like one big family and it felt great to be a part of it. This is when I knew this was the business for me.

I felt incredibly empowered to be consciously making positive changes, no matter how small the steps were at the start. All the steps were heading in the right direction, I loved the person I was becoming, and people started to notice. I had thrown myself in to personal development and slowly started to regain confidence by learning from others. I felt passionate about life and how I wanted to help so many others do the same.

Now, this journey wasn't all plain sailing and anyone in the network marketing industry will know, you have to get used to hearing the word no and learn to be resilient. Some will ignore you and some will be horrible about it. I have been in tears on many occasions throughout this journey. I've been at breaking point, feeling unworthy and not good enough to do this. I was thinking, *Is it really all worth it*? My answer is OMG yes. How can I deny people this opportunity to create the changes and share the experience that I have had? I knew I needed to learn more about being resilient. I needed to learn how to not take it all to heart, so that's what I did. I looked up to people who were successful, I listened and I read as much as I could. I had to break free from these thoughts and get out of my own head.

Fast forward to the beginning of this year, as I reflected on where I was, I asked myself, *Am I happy with what I have achieved? Am I where I want to be?* The answer was no. I had such a flying start to my business that I expected to be in a totally different place to where I actually was. I knew that the only person stopping me being where I wanted to be was me. I still had some growing to do and I still had to build on my confidence to become the person I aspired to be. My aim is to empower women and encourage them to become more confident. To flourish and live their best lives. To do that, I had to step out of my comfort zone.

When I came across the Femalepreneurs Academy and Neuro Linguistic Programming (NLP) combo, it had such a profound impact following on from timeline therapy with Jo Jo and Tash. I felt like everything I was storing up from past experiences had been lifted and I had released all that negativity from my past: fear, anger and worry. I felt empowered and I knew I was ready to make the next step in my journey. I wanted to help other women who had been like me, who had been scared to be the person they wanted to be, who felt like they were not good enough. Perhaps they had just lost their way but knew they were destined for great things. I knew NLP and timeline therapy were the answers to this and they were going to help bring the whole package together. Not only can I show people an amazing opportunity, I can also help support and guide them through challenges similar to those I have faced. I can help them become more confident, feel empowered and release all of their self-limiting beliefs, which stop them from reaching their goals. Enrolling in the NLP and timeline therapy course has given me that thing that I was missing. It helped me reach my goal to help as many people as possible.

If you are that woman who has been worn down, felt like they weren't good enough and letting past experiences rule their life, know that your past does not define you, you have everything within to be who and what you choose to be.

As I sit here finalising this chapter, I think back over the last six years and the journey I have been on. That broken, tired, worn out person is a distant memory. I have truly become the best version of me. My once dreamed of perfect family is nearly complete with our baby girl on the way and being only days away from completing our first family home together. I am truly living the life I had dreamed of. I have made it my mission to empower people to become confident and to flourish living their best life.

★★★

You can find Leanne here:

Www.facebook.com/leanne.willis.x
www.instagram.com/leanne_willis_x

# From Surviving to Thriving

## Lyndsey Shelley

*I'm Lyndsey shelley, a mother of two from Portsmouth, military wife of twelve years, retail manager turned network marketing professional. I dedicate this chapter to my husband, Ryan, my absolute hero, who no matter what life throws at us we stand together and work through it and is always my biggest supporter. To my children, Lily and Charlie, who have shown tremendous resilience throughout their little lives and make me so proud every single day. And my best friend, Claire, who is always there for me without judgement 100% of the time. And my mum and dad for their unconditional love and support in everything I do.*

I am writing this for the woman, mother, wife who has felt so completely broken by life, to show her that she can put herself back together again. To show her that she is important, she does matter and that it is not selfish to put yourself first. I hope by sharing my story of how I went from being young, ambitious and full of life to being suffocated by life pressure that it will help women like me push through their limiting beliefs and find their purpose and passion in life.

I smiled daily but it was all fake; inside I was broken and numb and every day just got up, smiled, ensured everyone else was okay and went back to sleep. Some days I couldn't even do that. In all honesty, that's what my life had looked like since 2010 when Ryan returned from Afghanistan. He was never the same man that returned and whilst I could have walked away and taken the children with me, I stayed and upheld my promise to look after the man I loved no matter how difficult it was some days. Some years after that tour of Afghanistan, which was literally one of the worst on record, Ryan was formally diagnosed with PTSD. And whilst a diagnosis is great, the support and road to recovery was a long one, which took its toll on all of us, especially me.

He left the military and ended up working within the ambulance service as part of HART (Hazardous Area Response Team). In all honesty, probably not the best move but it's what he was trained to do. I could feel myself sliding under the pressure and stress of trying to keep it all together for the kids and I reached out so many times for help but I never really got the response I was looking for. So, always resorted back to head down, keep busy.

I remember in 2015 getting to a really, really low point and issuing Ryan with an ultimatum. I couldn't take any more, we either did something drastic or I was out. It was this tough love that pushed Ryan to take up a residential placement at combat stress for his PTSD, where he had access to some of the leading clinicians in the industry. I was now riding solo with a seven and four year old whilst working full time, no contact, nothing. I went to the doctor and was given medication and that was as far as it went, as if it was going to make it all better. What it actually did was just numb any feeling I had left inside of me. The worst bit was I'd got to the point where I didn't care about me. I was in survival mode. As long as the kids and Ryan were safe and okay, I really had no regard for myself.

My confidence was shot, I couldn't get any lower, I stopped socialising, stopped talking to people, as I was fed up of putting on a brave face. I can count on a few fingers the number of people that saw past the fake smiles and actually asked how I was and I will always be grateful to those few people because they will never realise that on some horrible, horrible days when I put the kids to bed and sat there on my own at my lowest, how much their thoughts and kind words kept me going.

Ryan's PTSD did improve for a while and we got ourselves into a cycle we could live with. His medications were played around with and we just got on with it and accepted that although things were better he would never be the same. I guess we just accepted our lot. Sadly though, for me, I'd never been an accepting my lot kinda gal. I'd always been ambitious, wanted more from life, wanted to give my family the best of everything, but most of all I just wanted to feel like me again. I just wanted to feel happy, be happy and not live in the constant fear.

My coping mechanism was to be busy but that didn't

really work out well. Ryan was working HART shifts, and we high-fived on the doorstep most days/nights as we both went to work. If you looked up the definition of busy in the dictionary you would basically see our family photo. We lived for our holidays, the odd weekend away if we were both off, but truth is we were still just surviving.

Then in 2019 the best thing that could possibly have happened happened. This is going to sound super strange, so bear with me. Ryan relapsed. He had the best part of eight months off work and in true me style I got busy. I started working even harder to look after my family, Ryan was at home with the children and I took on an additional income role to plug the gap in his earnings. I was working with a financial education company and out probably two to four nights a week after finishing work, so I was probably working in excess of sixty to seventy hours a week, including admin and my full time retail management role.

Guess what, though? Just like before, this just wasn't sustainable. Now, don't get me wrong, I regret nothing. As a mother and a wife we have got to do what we have got to do, and that's exactly what I did. But in August, Ryan decided he would leave behind his career in the ambulance service and pursue other avenues. This was my opening for change too. I couldn't be supporting him and telling him if he doesn't like where he is to change it and take action if I wasn't doing it either, so I started looking for ways to escape the retail seven-day working week, including bank holidays and Christmas, and decided this would be my last Christmas in retail. I was prepared to work on myself, focus on my transferable leadership skills, really start looking at options and do what it took to achieve it. I didn't know how this was all going to happen, but when I make a decision, I always stand by it – I'm kinda stubborn like that!

So, I put it out to the universe and it's almost like at that point a little side door opened and in walked opportunity. But it was kind of in disguise. So it's October, the run up to Christmas, I've got a random lady who's been on my newsfeed a while and she pops up a post about selling perfume for Christmas. I thought of my sister straight away to earn a few pennies for Christmas and messaged her for the info. I sent the info to my sister and we decided to do it together. If I'm completely honest, I just didn't think I'd have time, so was just going to do it and hand-hold my sister and support her. So I signed us both up. It was completely free, so no risk, nothing to lose.

Anyway, later that day I jumped on a Zoom video call with the lady and when I saw the information on the business side of the perfume, the uncapped income and most importantly the time freedom it could give me, I realised this was it. This wasn't a little perfume business I was going to help my sister with, this was my way out. And, clear as day, I could see it. I could do it on my terms, when I wanted, all from my phone. I started to dream about what next Christmas might look like and got to work. For the first time in years, I was excited by the possibilities.

Then it all went a bit wrong. A few days in, the self-doubt kicked in, and the little person on my shoulder started to hold me to ransom: 'You can't do that, you aren't good enough, you're too busy, you've got a good secure job, you're being selfish, you're tired, you should rest, not start something else.' I started looking at the lady who had introduced me and decided actually I couldn't do it, it was just a pipe dream and whilst I could see lots of people were doing well, it wasn't for people like me. So I sent the message: "I'm really sorry to have wasted your time but this business isn't for me."

But it wasn't to be the end. It was a day off from work a few days later and I was just browsing Facebook as you do and a video popped up on one of the training groups the lady had added me to by a leading mindset coach in the network marketing industry. I sat and watched this video, and everything she said it was like she was talking to me. It was exactly how I was feeling. I really wanted to make the change and go for it but fear and self-doubt were holding me back.

Then I started to flip my thinking: What if? What if I could do it? What if the universe had sent me all of this to put me back on the right track? What if this was it and it was where I was meant to be? This mindset coach just talked to me and I sat there scribbling away and starting to work through some of the thoughts in my head, and decided I was exactly where I was meant to be. But I'd need help. Years of self-sacrifice, lack of confidence and self-worth, if I was going to go all in, I needed to get my head in the game. So I messaged her and signed up to her one to one mindset coaching.

Twelve weeks of uncovering so many emotions, realising that I'd made myself so unimportant and the fog started to lift. I had a new spring in my step, I was excited and full of energy and my confidence was going up and up and up. The self-development and rediscovering myself gave me a new lease of life. I didn't feel like I was getting up and going through the motions of the day, I jumped out of bed excited for the day ahead and my new "little perfume business" was going from strength to strength.

As my mindset and confidence grew, so did my business. The kids were happier, Ryan was happier and I realised that I wasn't the least important person in the family, I was the most important, the captain of the ship (pirate ship most days). If I was on my A-game, I could steer us anywhere and that's exactly what I did. Nine weeks into my business around my full time retail management role, I hit the first leadership level in the marketing plan. This came with big bonuses, a car paid for and an all-expenses-paid trip to the Maldives. I was literally pinching myself and just so grateful.

By this point, I was off my medication and starting to really feel alive again. It was a weird sensation to cry, and I mean proper cry with joy, with sadness at movies or in empathy for other people, because I'd just been so numb whilst taking my medication that emotions weren't really a thing. I have learned so much about myself on my journey and the best thing about it is that I'm surrounded by like-minded people who want more from life. I'm able to pass on my learnings and share my development journey to inspire and help others to give them that fire in their belly to allow them to achieve their goals too. I've found my purpose in life in terms of helping others and that just fills my heart so much.

I'm now at a point in my business that by the time this book is published I will have fulfilled my ultimate goal within a short ten months, and left my twenty-one year retail career behind me. I've tripled my monthly income and grown my business through the toughest economic times the country has seen for thirteen years. My goal has always been about time freedom and I know 100% that without doing the inner work and embracing the personal development journey, I wouldn't be where I am today. For anyone reading this maybe feeling stuck and in need of change in their life, my advice would be DO IT! Go to work on you, for you, you are the most important person in your life, it's never too late.

★★★

You can find Lyndsey here:

https://www.facebook.com/TheRetailRevolution/
https://www.facebook.com/lyndsey.shelley.3

# Life is for Living – Don't Settle for a Life Less Than You Deserve!

## Martha Bradford

*I dedicate this chapter to Miss Lynn Jane Tomelty, my biggest supporter in life. Whoever said time is a healer did not have a best friend like you. My Papa, Mr Andrew (to cut a long story short) Bradford. My beautiful daughters Cassidy Brooke and Layken and the little boy who stole all our hearts!*

I've heard her wrong. Imagine coming on a phone and telling me that. She's got this totally wrong! This can't be real. The tears were running down my face, cuddled into my two babies, totally broken. I couldn't breathe. You see, life can be so cruel at times. Some of us go through in a short space of time what others will never experience in an entire lifetime. That was the moment I received the call about my dad. I wanted my world to end there and then.

In a few short months, I'd lost my dad to suicide. My papa tragically died four weeks later in a house fire and shortly afterwards my marriage broke down. I was left with two young babies. Everyone I loved was slipping away!

The weeks shortly after that became one of the most traumatic times in my life. This cannot be happening! It must be a nightmare. I need to try and wake up. I may have taken too many painkillers and I'm probably delusional. Surely this is not real. I could hear my own screams and reality kicked in and I knew in that moment life would never be the same again.

A few hours prior, I'd been pacing the floors with the most excruciating toothache. I'd contemplated walking down to my grandparents' as I took the final two painkillers. Nothing was numbing the pain. Little did I know then that pain would be nothing compared to the pain I'd soon feel.

I heard a knock on the door and rushed voices downstairs. My husband came up with a look of horror and shock to tell me there had been the most horrific accident, that my grandparents' house was ablaze and I was to make my way to the hospital.

Papa was in a bad way. In hindsight, 'what if' are two of the biggest words ever! My papa was my biggest inspiration in life and worked hard for his family. He was a long-distance lorry driver and only came home on weekends. Yes, this was the very man when I proceeded as a teenager to tell him I wanted to be an air hostess, he told me I wouldn't even gain the qualifications to be a tattie howker at Toadhill Farm – if you're from Kilwinning you'll totally get me! Poor guys at Toadhill wouldn't know what'd hit them if I strolled up!

What can I say, I missed a lot of school and was probably a mother's worst nightmare. I walked away from school later with no qualifications and the teachers told me I'd never amount to anything in life. Maybe there was some truth in Andy Bradford's words that day!

I often felt I struggled to fit in. I had no real sense of belonging and, as a teenager, nights became fuelled with alcohol and drugs. I often thought friends became friends simply because they felt sorry for me. Strange, I know, but my insecurities and anxieties were my biggest problem.

I arrived at the hospital terrified to walk in the doors of the intensive care unit, petrified of what I'd see, but he simply looked as if he was in the most peaceful sleep with not a mark on his skin. He had the most perfect skin. Four weeks earlier, I'd been in that very hospital's morgue seeing my dad for the last time, and I whispered to my papa, 'I can't lose you too, you need to fight, Papa!'

Sadly, he passed away later that night and our hearts were broken forever. He'd often tell me, "Martha, the sky's the limit, reach for the stars," and those words have stayed with me my entire life. That was the start of antidepressants and allowing medication to suppress my thoughts and feelings, to numb me from the pain and to allow me from completely breaking.

They became my safety blanket for years. I remember not being able to lift my head from the kitchen table and feeling as though I was having an out-of-body experience. How can something that's been prescribed to make you feel better have such a horrible effect? I was told to push through the suicidal feelings and that after twelve weeks things should balance out.

Sounds silly, but I'd often go into little daydreams about the life I'd love to live, and then I'd pull myself back to reality, the self-limiting beliefs would kick in, then the voices from my childhood: "You'll never amount to anything!" would echo through my head. And quite rightly so, who was I to think for a minute someone like me – a single mum with no qualifications and two babies – could create success? My kids, Cassidy and Brooke, were my saviours back then and it's them who got me through the tough times. We don't know it at the time but it's during the worst times in our life that we become the strongest version of ourselves and it shapes us into the person we become today!

I became a mum at nineteen. My first-born baby girl was born premature, weighing less than a bag of sugar. She was the tiniest, most beautiful little thing I'd ever seen, and a new adventure began. We spent almost eight weeks between intensive care and then special care. Cassidy was only home a matter of weeks when I felt so ill. I remember my best friend popping a pregnancy test through the letterbox thinking it was hilarious, laughing while shouting, "I'm not coming in to witness the meltdown!"

The following July, Brooke was born. My life was my girls. I actually think twins would've been easier, but I wouldn't have changed it for the world.

I remarried and Layken was born a few years later. I applied for college many times over the years. Okay, let's keep it real, I applied for college five years in a row, but anxiety got the better of me. I lacked so much confidence and literally had no self esteem. I'd get the call or email to attend an interview and act as though I never received it. On reflection, I think when you're constantly told you'll never amount to anything, it becomes instilled within you.

Fear of failure held me back for years and fear of what people thought would actually halt me in my steps. Even an invite to a wedding would totally freak me out with the thought of walking into a place with so many people I'd never met before.

Martha, this needs to stop! I had a complete meltdown. I needed to overcome this. I spent a fortune on counselling, talking therapies, hypnosis, but still nothing helped. I went to the GP for advice to be told I was suffering from depression. No shit, Sherlock, as if I didn't know that! However, a new label was placed on my medical record that day: social anxiety.

People would often think I was the life and soul of the party but OMG they had no idea. Inside, I was crumbling with anxiety. Wine would ease the pain and allow me to have a little more confidence. I got so fed up with putting a face on for everyone when inside I felt broken. I had worked since leaving school, from pubs to caring, but I wanted more and needed to find a way out of this vicious cycle I was creating inside my head.

I remember feeling pretty proud of myself during my graduation, thinking, *Well, Andy, I eventually gained those qualifications*. Maybe not an air hostess, but still, a qualification is a qualification, even though I suffered a near-death experience when I was asked to read aloud in class! It's fair to say public speaking was not my thing but I gained enough confidence to successfully complete my college course after only five years of holding myself back. Go me…

You see, we are our own worst critics in life. We hold ourselves back through fear and what others think. When I think back now, if I was in this place I'm in now five years ago, there'd be no stopping me! I still have my moments, but all the treatments and medication in the world are nothing in comparison: the real magic starts when you start to believe in yourself and have a little self love and a vision that's greater than your excuses.

I've always been passionate about making a difference in people's lives. I began working with kids who were accommodated in the care system and absolutely loved my job. I loved making a positive difference. I could totally relate to these kids and the trauma they'd been through and the reasons for the challenging behaviours. Been there, done that and wore the T-shirt! Although I loved the job, I still wasn't satisfied. I still wanted more. I was always searching for something, but I didn't know quite what that something was. I was spending more time with kids who were in the care system than my own and something really had to change. I don't know if it was luck or fate or a little guardian angel but things were about to change.

In life I'm such a big believer that a closed mind will cost you an absolute fortune.

I was standing in my mum's pub and the fear was setting in. I can't do this. I was launching my business. I had around twenty-five people attending. I made it very clear under no circumstances could I do launch nights, planning sessions or speak to more than three people at once. Hell, I actually couldn't do any of the things I needed to do to grow a long-term sustainable business, but I had this little voice telling me, 'You can do this!' A bottle of rosé wine later and still my nerves were shattered.

You see, when I say I was nervous, you might not fully comprehend the level I actually mean. Lorna took the lead and we made it through a successful first launch. That was five years ago. I'd never heard of the industry before and genuinely thought it was a pyramid scheme or some sort of scam, but I took the time to understand the business model. The one thing I had in my favour was I was open to taking a look. I'd been approached a few times and, if I'm completely honest, as I followed a few people online and watched their success unfold, I'd often tell these people, 'No, it's not for me,' when deep inside I was desperate to jump on board, get to work and make it happen.

But yep, you guessed it, all those old anxieties came flooding back and I was paralysed with fear. It was almost as though I had two people fighting inside my head on repeat. Martha, go for it, you'll be amazing and the other shouting, You'll never amount to anything in life, and laughing.

Depression and anxiety was still a part of daily life. It's not something you can switch on and off as you please. It's something you learn to live with. You learn to not fight the bad days, accept you're having an off day and remember tomorrow is a new day.

Twelve weeks after becoming an independent business owner, I'd replaced my income plus some, decided to resign from my position and went full time in my network marketing business. This was when my true passion for health and self-development kicked in. Back then we were sold into a lie that we could work our business online a few hours a day and create success. The reality being I spent most of my day stuck to my phone. I was doing launch nights for the team every night, driving all over the UK. An industry that was to allow me so much more time freedom was actually driving me away from my family.

My first company taught me the basic skills I needed, it taught me that not everyone will understand your journey and that's okay. It taught me that you need to be consistent and persistent and stay focused on your journey and never compare yourself to others.

In June 2016 was the day a lot changed inside me! I lost my best friend, my sister, my go to person through it all, the only person who truly got me. My biggest supporter in life! The one who always had my back! I'd been doing a planning session with one of the team that morning and she'd called. I remember thinking, I'll call her back, as I then made my way to the hair salon. I'll never forget the look on Erin's face when she walked into the salon to tell me her mum had just passed away. A piece of my heart broke that day and "what if" was all I could think. There's not a day goes past where you're not in my thoughts. Sometimes I look up and smile and simply know that was you guiding me.

My next company took me all over the world with the team, Milan, Poland, Haiti, Florida and the Caribbean. I met some truly amazing people during this time and met some not so truly amazing people. Losing Lynn made me realise that life is far too short to not do what makes you happy. Could you imagine lying on your deathbed having lived a life of regret? Follow your dreams and always do what makes you happy.

I was told by a psychic that a little bundle of joy was being sent to mend a broken heart and soon afterwards I fell pregnant with Lincoln and my little ray of sunshine was born. I was back to building a business around a baby. James and I had been struggling for some time and split after more than twenty years together. People stay in marriages when they fall out of love or that make them unhappy or stay in jobs where they feel overworked and underpaid simply because fear of change cripples them. We only get one chance at this thing called life and it's up to us to make the most of it.

Within my time in the industry I've touched on a few companies and I've witnessed the good and the bad but after four years I was starting to feel the pressure a little and when people stop winning it's time to decide where you're going. I was so fed up with that whole self-consumption model where the only real volume coming through was struggling reps on smart ship every month with no real customer volume. I did not want to bring people in to then fail. If you don't have a strong customer base, you don't have a business.

A few things happened during this period, which left me burned out, deflated. Sometimes we simply trust in the wrong people and make the wrong decisions and life can seem a little overwhelming. An industry that had given me so much was now starting to cripple me and my path was unclear.

I sat contemplating life and was wondering what path to take. For a few months I cried and felt like an absolute failure. I was lost and all over the place. I was an absolute emotional wreck. Where would my income come from? What would I do next? Lots of questions I couldn't answer. My future was so uncertain. I'd been approached by various people all promoting their opportunity but I'd lost my passion. Would I go back to social work... what would I do?

After lots of chatting with someone I'd followed for years, she asked me to come back – to a better way of working, to a community where everyone was winning, regardless of previous experience. I sat contemplating for weeks and then decided if I was coming back it was time to level up and help as many people as I possibly could. I was done playing small and a new energy and confidence was created! It's amazing what happens when you surround yourself with the right people at the right time.

We hear it all the time but when you fully commit to becoming a better version of you, everything starts aligning. The universe always has your back. The right people walk into your life. What's been created in such a short space of time is nothing short of incredible. We're now part of the fastest growing team in the company history and smashing records. This is the way the industry should be, the simplicity of building a business through sharing a code leveraging social media while creating memories with my family.

Always lead with integrity and honesty! Become an expert in solving people's problems. I'm all about making this industry a better place and helping others do the same!

Helping people overcome self-limiting beliefs and unleashing the magic within is what drives me forward! The gig economy is massively on trend and social retail is changing the game in the online space with more people now open to a new way of working.

I've realised that it's not so much anxiety, I'm a true empath. I walk into a room and pick up different energies. If someone is sad or nervous, I pick that up. I also pick up when someone is not genuine and a narcissist, but that's another story.

I started off with no confidence and very little self-belief but I had a passion that was bigger than my excuses! We face many challenges and traumas in life, and some hit us harder than others. It's how we adapt and evolve that's key to any future success in life! I hope whoever reads this book can take a little inspiration and guidance knowing that no matter what life throws at you or where you come from there is light at the end of the tunnel. We are all born with greatness inside, it's up to us to unleash it.

Feel the fear and do it anyway! Remember, we

only get one chance at this thing called life. Be open to new opportunities in life, don't be so sceptical. Find something that could quite literally change all your tomorrows but most importantly don't stop dreaming. Dreams do come true if you simply believe!

★★★

You can find Martha here:

https://www.facebook.com/martha.templeton.7777

# The Road to Light

## Melanie Jack

*I dedicate this book to all the people that were in my life who caused me both pain and joy, for every experience has shaped who I am today.*

It was a hot summer evening and I was upstairs with Mum. I'd just got out of the bath and was in my pyjamas ready for bed. Me and my older sister were arguing again, about a doll this time! Mum said, "Girls, that's enough! Time to go to sleep now, goodnight, love you both," and she shut the door. I remember it being far too hot, that I had to kick the blankets off me, and continued to toss and turn as I could not sleep.

Suddenly, the front door slammed. He was home. I heard him banging around and going into the other bedroom. They started arguing again, my mum said, "Look at you, drunk again."

I would put the pillow over my head to try to block out the shouting. Then I heard screaming. I got out of my bed and ran to open my mum's door. There was blood everywhere from my mum's nose.

"Dad, please, stop, leave Mum alone!" I screamed.

This was a regular thing and went on for many years. Eventually, he would vent his drunken anger on us children too.

Most of my younger years were a combination of psychological and physical abuse that sadly became the norm for me. My dad was an alcoholic and I witnessed domestic violence growing up. I was raped at the age of seventeen. These times were my deep and dark nights of the soul. My life continued to spiral out of control.

I was a lost, vulnerable young girl, not knowing who I was or where I was going in life. Eventually I moved away from the area and tried to start again. I met some new friends and almost felt a belonging. I really looked up to this friend and she took care of me. I moved in with her and she became my role model who inspired me to be just like her. She had nice cars and lots of money. I mirrored her and, without even being aware, I became involved with the wrong crowd, drugs, money and fast cars. This new lifestyle took me from a world of poverty to affluence. I was like a celebrity, everyone knew of me, I felt untouchable! Shopping when I wanted, buying all the designer clothes, Gucci, Chanel and Dior. I was living a luxury life!

This, however, was extremely dangerous. I was involved with a lot of notorious people from the underworld and felt I had to always be one step ahead; one mistake and I could be dead or in prison. Deep down, I wanted out from this kind of life. I was always looking over my shoulder, living in fear, but the money kept me there. Shopping in Harrods and living in Marbella,

I thought this was the life that everyone wanted, to be happy. But I might as well have been in prison as I was a prisoner in my own mind. There's that saying, 'money doesn't bring happiness', and guess what, that was so true.

It was late that cold evening, and I was at my boyfriend's mother's house. It was around ten o'clock, and I decided to get my head down. I went upstairs into the spare room and went to bed. I put my phone on vibrate under my pillow and started to drift off. Suddenly, I was woken by the vibration of the phone underneath my pillow. I pulled it out and the screen lit up in the dark room; it was him. My heart started to race, my anxiety kicked in and my thoughts were running wild. The palms of my hands started to sweat, I went into complete panic mode.

I answered the phone. "Hello," I said.

Immediately he was shouting down the phone: "You slag, where are you?"

"I'm at your mum's," I replied.

He continued to abuse me down the phone and accuse me of sleeping with other men. This was a regular pattern of behaviour when he was high on substances. I put the phone down as I could not continue to listen to any more abuse. He continued to call my phone, but I ignored it.

I started to drift off again but was woken by the sound of the door. His heavy footsteps creaking against the floorboards got louder and louder until eventually he swung open the door and barged right in, grabbing me with brute force, pushing me onto the bed, shouting, "Where are your car keys, you slag!"

My head was telling me to just give him the blasted keys, but my heart which loved and cared for him so much was telling me don't, he'll end up somewhere dead in a ditch.

When I refused to give him the keys, I saw that look in his eyes. The voice was saying, *Run, quick, he's going to hurt you*. I found an opportunity and immediately ran into his mum's room and shut the door. Bear in mind, he was a big muscular man and extraordinarily strong. He kicked the door down and came at me whilst in the back his mum and little sister were screaming. He was attacking me with some sharp object all over my body. He then went for my face. This is where I tried to protect myself with my hand and next thing I knew he got my keys and ran. All I could see was blood everywhere and lots of screaming going on in the house. Panic mode kicked in. I was not sure where the blood was coming from, I was in complete shock! I thought, *This is it, I am going to die*.

The ambulance arrived and I was rushed into A&E where they operated on me. I was one of the lucky ones once again. He just missed my main artery and I was on the mend. My friends and family came to the hospital. They were really angry. I didn't even want to face them because I knew exactly what they were going to say. "Next time he's going to kill you, you've got to leave him, you can't do this any more, he's crazy and capable of anything. When are you going to realise? When it's too late and you're dead." They were right, this wasn't the first time.

I remember when we lived out in the country in the middle of nowhere in a beautiful little cottage with a river going through the garden with no neighbours for miles. This was the time when I was nearly drowned to death in the bath. I remember this day like it was yesterday, gasping for breath, thinking that was it. I was screaming for help, but no one could hear me. This was going on for many years, but enough was enough, surely.

I had to consciously make the biggest decision of my life. I had to do the right thing, so I spoke to the police and said I would go ahead and go to court. The big day came, and I was so nervous. As much as I knew it was the right thing to do, my heart was telling me the opposite. This was a very stressful time for me and all the family, but we saw it through. Finally, the day of the verdict came. The verdict came out 'not guilty' and part of me was still in shock. Deep down, I sighed with relief. (I loved him and didn't want to see him spend many more years in prison.) I wasn't a saint and was just as bad as him many times. I would attack him, as I had so much jealousy and anger built up due to the conditioning of my upbringing over the years, which came out in all my relationships.

This time I thought I would do the right thing for both of us and I stayed clear of him for a few months. But not for long. Like an addiction, I went back to him. My heart was too pure and not like everyone else. I knew him, the real person, when he was not on substances, how kind and generous he really was, so again we got back together. Before I knew it, he went back to prison, but this time it was a blessing in disguise. If he had not gone to prison, we would have stayed in a relationship where we kept hurting each other and one of us would have ended up killing the other.

But something powerful happened. He called me one evening from prison, he had broken down crying, saying how sorry he was and how he was finished and done with that life. He started to change daily, something was different, but I just could not put my finger on it. Then he told me what happened to him in his prison cell. He said that he prayed that night and then went to sleep and he had a spiritual experience where he was vibrating from head to toe in pure light.

This is when the real journey began. He called me on to a visit and said that I had to choose between him or the lifestyle I was living. This was the hardest and the biggest decision of my life… but thank God I chose life.

Having the courage to give up my old lifestyle and start again from rock bottom was huge, but I had the strength and courage to push through.

During this time, I had to go deep within myself, reading many self-help books every day. I was growing more and more, learning about me and who I was and how I could finally love myself before I could even love anyone else. I had to detach myself from my ego as I was addicted to the materialistic lifestyle.

There is resilience in us all. And most importantly, there is our Creator (call it God, Universe, Buddha,

Allah or whatever you believe in). When you truly believe with your whole heart and have complete faith that the Creator has got you, then he will work for you.

I finally got in touch with the God within my true self that I am. I started practicing my daily rituals: gratitude, praying, meditation and positive affirmations. These are three elements that I live by on a day-to-day basis, growing stronger spiritually and mentally every day! Positive affirmations have the power to resonate deep into your consciousness and truly manifest your dreams!

This is where my inner journey started, retraining the subconscious mind and eliminating any negative past experiences through meditation and a supportive new belief system. The first step in creating change was believing it was possible and surrounding myself with positive reinforcement. I created a master plan and identified my core values and motivations. In short, you can achieve just about anything if you first take the time to re-programme your subconscious mind!

In order for me to shift on a new level I had to change my diet, eating healthy food, exercising and taking care of my mind, body and soul. All the above was a contributing factor towards change and how to recreate a new life of endless possibilities.

Through this process, day by day, my light got brighter and brighter. However, this was a painful process. I had to learn to forgive myself before anyone else, but I had determination to succeed. I can look back and be grateful for my life experiences and journey, as this has made me the strong independent woman I am today.

## The Big Day

He was finally released from prison. We got married, and this was the happiest moment of our lives. Not everyone was happy, as they thought I was mad to marry him and that he would not change. We were judged by many and lost people we thought were friends in the process.

I know what you must be thinking: how is this couple still together? The relationship was so unhealthy and that is so true, and I would not advise any couple to stay in a relationship so toxic, but seek professional help.

We get that not everyone is going to resonate with our story. However, we believe this was a supernatural divine intervention and we honestly believe that everything happens for a reason, good or bad. We have taken our mess and turned it into a message to inspire change.

We continued our journey and vowed to live a life of self-discovery and service towards helping others to find their true self and discover the power within.

Life really is a roller coaster, so whether you are up or down, remember that it's just temporary and it's all part of the journey. Truthfully, when you decide something with your heart, the universe lays out the path for you.

Since then, I have proudly co-created two companies, RoadLight Ltd and 7RoadLight non-profit Community

Interest Company. The mission is to reach out to as many lives and help them to discover their true human potential. I lead a team of mentors at Her Majesty's Prison to support and educate people with life and social skills and help them heal from their trauma. The aim is to help the most challenging individuals develop a positive identity and thrive for positive change.

I finally feel free to share this with the rest of the world to help you feel empowered, giving you a hope for your future, to inspire you to make the transition, no matter what you've been through or are going through. You can do anything you want in life and don't let anyone hold you back, including yourself. To know that your past does not define who you are but shapes your character and gives you the strength and power to overcome all adversities. I believe that every person has the potential to become the best version of themselves. I want you to know how special, unique and gifted you are, to finally be who you were created to be with a passion and purpose to step into the best version of yourself.

> *"Approximately 1% of domestic abusers that really want and try are able to change. Note that it does not say that 1% of all abusers change but just the 1% that really desire to do the work."*

It is important to understand that I was the lucky one. Had Dwayne not had his spiritual awakening in prison, we most likely would have continued to live in an abusive relationship that would have eventually ended up as the following statistic: "Domestic abuse leads to more than 30,000 deaths per year worldwide."

So, if you are suffering from a domestic abuse relationship, please do seek professional help and call the National Domestic Abuse Helpline on: 0808 2000 247

★★★

You can find Melanie here:

Website www.roadlight.co.uk
www.7roadlight.co.uk
Facebook: Melanie Jack
Instagram: meljack7
Linkedin: Melanie Jack

# The Fire Within
## Monique Sveinsson

*I am writing this to my husband, Agust, who inspires me and encourages me in all my crazy pursuits. To my two fabulous children, Isabelle and Sienna, who make me want to do more and be better. Girls, I want to show you anything is possible. And finally, I dedicate this chapter to my daughter Rosa, the daughter whom we didn't get to know, who was too wonderful for this world. Thanks to you, Angel, you made the fire in me explode and ensured I did what I was meant for in this world.*

> "The world may never notice if a rose doesn't bloom, or even pause to wonder if the petals fall too soon. But every life that ever forms, or ever comes to be, touches the world in some small way for all eternity."

### January 2014

We stepped out of the car and the cold wind hit my face, freezing the tears that were already flowing. There were two suited men standing in front of me, asking my husband and I if we wanted to hold the box. I shook my head and held tightly onto my husband. I could barely feel my legs. We slowly followed the men down the gravel path and into the garden ahead of us. My family were all standing there, looking at my husband and I with tear-filled faces. I could see the pain in their eyes and it made me hold my husband tighter than ever. The men gently placed the box on the ground, and I laid the most beautiful bunch of white roses onto the box. No one said anything for what seemed like forever, we just stood in silence. We were standing in the cemetery in an area called the baby garden. Within that box was our daughter, our Rosa, our little girl who was born sleeping and was clearly far too beautiful to be in this world.

I never thought I'd recover, I never thought I would be able to carry on, I wanted to give up. I couldn't believe this had happened to me, to us. As I lay in bed the days and weeks after we said goodbye to Rosa, I questioned life over and over again: why me, why us, what had we done to deserve this? It just didn't seem fair. The day I lost Rosa was the day I lost a piece of myself!

I blamed myself for what had happened, blaming it on my life, my busy lifestyle, the nature of my work! At the time I was working on the London show *War Horse*. I loved the show, I loved the people and I loved my work. I was Stage Manager on one of the UK's biggest shows and I was in my element, organising and planning, day in, day out! But I was tired, I was working long hours and I was pregnant! I also had a two-year-old daughter at home who needed me. I was trying to juggle it all, a two-year-old, seventy-hour working weeks, childcare and a musician husband on tour, all whilst being pregnant. So yes, I did blame myself for what happened.

★

From a very young age I always had what I considered to be an entrepreneurial spirit. Although I was extremely fortunate coming from a well-balanced and happy home life where money wasn't particularly an issue, I knew I wanted to make my own money early on, I wanted control over my finances. So, starting at the age of thirteen, I walked a dog for £2 an hour, then started babysitting, had a 'Saturday job' in a clothes shop, then managed that clothes shop for the family when they went away for the entire summer! This gave me an amazing understanding of business by the age of sixteen! Don't worry, this chapter isn't going to be a reading of my CV, honestly, there is a point to all this! Even though by eighteen I knew I was going to work in the theatre and the arts, I had cottoned on that theatre was going to be my passion project, there was very little money in it but I loved it so I'd need to do 'other things' to top up my income. So on I went, working in the theatre, working on some life-changing shows with life-changing experiences and life-changing people, but always thinking 'what else, what else can I do, this job isn't for life, there has to be more'! But I carried on. I carried on for twenty years, in fact, working the long hours with small paycheques, all the time topping up my money by working in restaurants, bar work and shop work. I even started a magazine franchise, nearly ran a ballet school (that's another story but unfortunately that didn't go to plan), sold double glazing, catalogue distribution, you name it, I did it! Not one person could ever question that I didn't work hard! But in all the time of doing this, I didn't feel satisfied. I knew I had more to give, I had more value to give to the world and I had more to give myself. Please don't misunderstand me, don't think it was all about the money; it was never about making as much money as possible, it was about personal satisfaction. There was a fire inside me, an energy and a longing to be the best I could be, and I had to keep going until I found what I was looking for. On paper, I had it all. By the age of twenty-four I was a home owner, I had a great career, great friends and one hell of a lifestyle. However, my ambition to do something else was high but I just couldn't ever seem to place my finger on what it was.

★

So back to January 2014. Unfortunately for us, the sadness didn't end there. After a long recovery both physically and mentally after losing Rosa (I should say here mentally is very loose, you never get over losing a child, you somehow learn to accept but you can't and shouldn't ever forget!), life had resumed some semblance of normality. I went back to work on the show and Agust, my husband, went back to touring life. The cast and crew of *War Horse* were an amazing support and I laughed like a hyena most days, yet things were not the same on the inside. To most it seemed like we'd got it together and we were moving on, but I was grieving, and I was frustrated! The fire had somehow dwindled and I felt lost. Something in me wasn't right and I couldn't place it. I was longing for more in my career and working life and I wanted a second baby. I was existing, certainly not living!

## August 2014

Later that year, we tried again for another baby and, happy days, I fell pregnant. Sadly, the little girl we were carrying did not make it and I had a rather nasty miscarriage at thirteen weeks. After having already lost Rosa and now another baby, I was low, feeling a devastation and at a loss like I'd never known. After the surgery, which I'd unfortunately had to have, I was at home recovering, feeling extremely down, realising the likelihood of bringing a brother or sister into the world for Isabelle was disappearing and it felt awful. I stayed in my bed for days, I'd lost my sparkle, my love of life and my strength. I just didn't feel the same anymore. As I lay there, the same few thoughts whizzed round and round my head. 'There may only be one child, I just have Isabelle, but I need to appreciate her. I need to be there for her.' Plus, I knew I still hadn't fulfilled my ambitions, whatever they were. I still wanted more from my life, but what? What could I do that would see me be with Isabelle but by doing that it would take me away from the only job I loved? It was a huge wrench. Isabelle might be my only chance to be the mum I felt I should be, and I (in my mind) wasn't doing it adequately. She had one year until she started school and I just knew I wanted to spend that year with her!

Later that morning, after another painkiller-induced sleep, I lay there browsing my phone on Facebook, the time-zapping app that we all know and love. I saw an advert! The advert that changed my life, the advert that gave me a new strength, the advert that made me want to get better, the advert that allowed me to be mum to my Isabelle!

"Are you fed up of working long hours, do you want to be at home more with your children, do you wish to earn an income from home, working hours to suit you? I have five places available for mums who are looking for a work from home opportunity."

*What is this?* I thought. This seemed like all my questions were being answered right here in this tiny little Facebook post. My intuition, my gut, my everything was telling me I needed to answer this. I needed to be one of the five. I needed to explore it, I needed to investigate. I answered the message and within two hours I was dragging my broken body out of bed to meet a lady I didn't know for a coffee. I could barely walk but I knew I needed to be there!

A couple of hours later, I came home feeling light as a feather and on cloud nine! I came into the house screaming to my husband, 'This is it! I've found my way out! I've cracked it, THIS IS AMAZING!' I literally couldn't believe it, I'd been shown a business model which could be the ultimate thing that would change mine and my family's life.

Well, many of us have been there and seen these types of messages, we may have even been sent one. That message was inviting me to join a well-known network marketing company. I met the lady who became my sponsor and she invited me into the heady world of MLM. I couldn't believe my luck. Literally everything I wanted was right there.

Later that month, I kissed goodbye to the wonderful *War Horse* cast and crew and stepped away from the theatre for good to run my business and be at home with my baby girl Isabelle. I threw myself into the business, learning as much as I could, absorbing every bit of training and becoming a complete product of my product. I did everything I was told, and I loved every moment of my journey. Of course, people laughed at me and criticised me for doing one of those 'pyramid things', but I had a laser-like focus and no one was going to stop me. I must admit, on the inside, it did bother me having people be so negative and some so downright nasty, I'd never seen anything quite like it, but I carried on through the adversity and animosity and quickly worked out who my cheerleaders were. You see, I was totally naive to network marketing, I just didn't understand why people could be so negative. Could they not see what I saw? But regardless of their opinions, I carried on. I was home and spending time with my little girl, so their opinions just didn't count! In my theatre job I had spent years shrugging my shoulders to people saying, 'Ah Monique, it's so lovely you get to pursue your hobby, but when are you going to get a real job?!' It was only when I made a success in theatre that people started to take notice. I knew network marketing was going to be the same! All the time, I thought WATCH ME!

You see, the combination of working like a dog my whole life and the baby battles I endured, made me one hell of a tough girl. When you lose a child, you have to develop a sink or swim attitude. I was not going to sink. Of course, there were down days, of course there were moments – how could there not be? – but I wasn't going to drown! **NO WAY!**

What happened over the next few years truly became life changing. The belief in myself to achieve more grew day by day, my resilience increased to a whole new level and my eyes opened. I felt a bit like the boy in the film *The Sixth Sense* who said, 'I see dead people,' instead all I could see was opportunity. It was everywhere, I wanted to do everything!

## JULY 2015

In 2015 I gave birth to my second daughter, despite thinking it wasn't going to happen. I'm extremely lucky, it did. It wasn't an easy pregnancy, as you can well imagine, but it was one that ended well and we had our beautiful Sienna against all the odds. Even though we discovered with Rosa that there was something fundamentally wrong, I still believe my anxiety and stress levels played a part in her tragedy. This time by being relaxed and open-minded to so much more, things turned out really well and it actually shows in Sienna's personality. She is resilient, feisty and strong, yet the most chilled out, no stress little girl you could know. I don't believe for a moment there is a coincidence there!

In business, I went from strength to strength. With my powerhouse of a husband behind me, we learned everything we could and launched a planner business for network marketers: Network Marketing Manager. I saw a gap in the market and took it. People were joining network marketing and, like me, many were mums. These mums struggled to get organised and were becoming stressed and overwhelmed. They were then quitting their business saying it didn't work.

My theatre career had given me such a high level of organisation, I knew with the right tool I could help those people and give them more time in their life, just like I had wanted. The planner business expanded into The Perfect Planner Company by selling productivity stationery for entrepreneurs and home-based business owners. We have received rave reviews from across the globe. I was in my element. It has been with grit, determination and so much stamina we did this, creating our empire that has given us that six-figure business we wanted while being at home and being a mum.

Is it hard? Hell yes! Do I have days where I want to throw it all away and go back to getting my weekly paycheque? Occasionally, yes! Would I do it, though? Absolutely not. Why, because I now know my dream of giving back to the world, my dream of being an entrepreneur has been achieved. I am willing to ignore the hard days, I am willing to accept that we are on a roller coaster and I am willing to do anything to make mine and my family's lives a better one! I haven't finished yet, though. I have so much more to give and will continue to do so. See, the life of an entrepreneur means you never settle. It's almost like a drug, you can't stop, because once you've opened your eyes, once you start to realise there is more out there, once you use the sadness in your life and channel it into the positive, you become unstoppable!

There is always a light at the end of the tunnel, you just have to keep looking because believe me, it is there. Just don't give up, stay true to you and do what your intuition tells you and you will find your fire within.

★★★

You can find Monique here:

Www.perfectplannerco.com
Www.instagram.com/perfect planner.company
Www.facebook.com/nmmanager

www.ingramcontent.com/pod-product-compliance
Lightning Source LLC
Chambersburg PA
CBHW072030230526
45466CB00020B/1207